Month-by-Month Reading, Writing, and Phonics for Kindergarten

Second Edition

by

Dorothy P. Hall

and Patricia M. Cunningham

Carson-Dellosa Publishing Company, Inc.

Greensboro, North Carolina

In 1997, we wrote *Month-by-Month Reading and Writing for Kindergarten*. We did not call it *Month-by-Month Phonics for Kindergarten* because we believed that at this grade level, phonics was best taught with students' names and reviewed while reading Morning Messages, during the shared reading of big books, and when young children stretch out words, listen for sounds they know, and write them. In this revised edition, we do those same activities, but we want teachers and parents to know that we are working on phonics in a way that makes sense to young students. We stress the phonemic awareness activities in the book—just in case some teachers missed them. We also move up some of the activities to the first month, especially the Morning Message because it is so powerful for young children. Besides, most teachers do not want to wait until December to do the Morning Message—nor should they!

We hope that kindergarten teachers will find this book a compromise between scripted "phonics" programs that ask teachers to say and do things that do not make sense to young students (or to those of us who are older!) and other "developmental" programs that want teachers to wait, or postpone instruction, until all students are ready. We think that reading, writing, and phonics can be taught in a multilevel way in which different students learn different things depending on their various levels of literacy learning. We also hope that teachers and students continue to have fun as they learn!

This book is dedicated to kindergarten teachers everywhere and especially to those teachers who have shared ideas with us and whose superb teaching inspired the writing of this book.

Dottie and Pat

Credits

Editors

Jennifer Weaver-Spencer
Joey Bland

Layout Design

Van Harris

Inside Illustrations

Lori Jackson

Cover Design

Van Harris

Cover Photos

© 1997 Comstock, Inc.
© 2002 Brand X Pictures

Table of Contents

Table of Contents

Phonics Instruction in Kindergarten

How do you feel about the phonics part of your kindergarten curriculum? Do you look forward to teaching your students about letters and sounds each day? More importantly, how do your students feel about learning phonics? Do they look forward to their daily dose of phonics instruction? If thinking about these questions makes you visualize stacks of worksheets, workbook pages, flash cards, and phonics drills, you need this book.

Are your students having **fun** learning about letters and sounds? Do you **actively engage** students in learning, or do you rely on worksheets and workbook pages? Can all of your students—including students with special needs and English language learners—participate and achieve some level of success and satisfaction from phonics activities? Are the phonics lessons taught in a way that maximizes transfer and application to the reading and writing that students will be asked to do?

Month-by-Month Reading, Writing, and Phonics for Kindergarten teaches the same "what" as other kindergarten phonics programs but in a very different way. All of the activities in *Month-by-Month Reading, Writing, and Phonics for Kindergarten* were designed to be consistent with the research about engagement, motivation, and transfer. Young learners are engaged and motivated when they perceive an activity as fun or enjoyable and when they are able to successfully participate. Learners are engaged and motivated when they can actively participate—physically and mentally—in the activity. Transfer occurs when the activity in which the strategies are taught is closely connected to the activity in which learners need to actually use the strategies. Here are some examples of how the "what" of kindergarten phonics is taught in a fun, active, and success- and transfer-oriented way.

Students learn and review the 26 letter sounds connected to their names and the names of their classmates. They learn and recite tongue twisters to review all of the beginning sounds. They listen to familiar nursery rhymes and new rhyming books and find the rhyming words early in the year or round up rhymes later in the year. Kindergartners learn to use these rhyming patterns to read and spell new words in Making Words lessons. When they are writing, they learn to stretch out words, listen for the sounds, and write these sounds.

Phonics instruction is an essential part of a beginning reading program in kindergarten. Learning and reviewing letters and sounds should not be boring and repetitive, especially for students who come to school already knowing all of the letters and sounds! It should not be too difficult for students who come to school with few literacy experiences. You can teach phonics in ways that are not boring, repetitive, or far removed from the reading and writing kindergartners are asked to do in school. Phonics should not be taught in isolation, so each month of this book describes ways to do real reading and writing with kindergarten students. The activities in this book might even change your answers to the questions in the first paragraph.

Introduction

It's the first day of kindergarten! For some parents, today is the day when they separate from their child and watch her begin a journey toward literacy. Whatever the preparation, it is a big day for both parents and children! The children, as little as they are, know that this is a big day. Some are nervous and scared; but almost all are excited.

Teachers are excited too, and most are still apprehensive, even after years of teaching kindergarten. What will the parents expect from kindergarten this year? Everyone knows that what happens in kindergarten will make a big difference for these students!

The reading and writing activities in this book will help all children begin or continue their literacy journeys. The activities described are **multilevel**. A multilevel activity includes **multiple things to be learned** and **multiple ways for children, no matter what their stages of development, to move forward.**

These activities are also developmentally appropriate—the curriculum is carefully framed on knowledge of children's physical, social, and intellectual growth. It is based on what children need to learn and what is known about how children learn.

A developmentally appropriate kindergarten is like a good home where children learn through playing, watching, listening, acting, reading or pretend reading, and writing or pretend writing. It is a place where children can explore their environment, ask questions, and answer questions. It is a place where the teacher acts like a parent: reading to the children and talking about stories; writing for the children and allowing them to write for different purposes; exploring the community with students on field trips; and talking about those experiences together. It is a place where children learn about familiar and unfamiliar topics (usually called themes) and learn about what interests them most—themselves. Most importantly, it is a place where children learn that reading provides both enjoyment and information and where they develop the desire to learn how to read and write.

Learning how to read and write appears effortless for some children. For others, it is a struggle. Findings from emergent literacy research have demonstrated that children who easily learn how to read have had a variety of home experiences with reading and writing that enables them to profit from school literacy instruction ("Emergent Literacy" by Elizabeth Sulzby and William M. Teale, *Handbook of Reading Research*, Vol. II, 1991). From these experiences, children develop critical understandings that are the building blocks of their success.

Unfortunately, not all children have had home experiences through which they can develop these understandings. In developmentally appropriate kindergartens, teachers provide a variety of experiences that simulate as closely as possible those at-home reading and writing experiences so that all children develop critical understandings.

The goals of a developmentally appropriate kindergarten are to accept all children where they are and to take them forward on their literacy journeys.

Phonemic awareness is the realization that spoken words are made up of sounds. These sounds (phonemes) are not separate and distinct. Phonemic awareness has many levels and includes the abilities to decide whether spoken words rhyme, to know what spoken words would result from removing sounds, to segment words into sounds, and to blend sounds into words. Phonemic awareness is one of the best predictors of a child learning how to read (National Reading Panel, 2000).

Phonics can be defined simply as the understanding of the relationship between letters and sounds. *Put Reading First* (Armbruster, Lehr, and Osborne, 2001) summarizes the findings of the National Reading Panel and says, "Teachers explicitly and systematically instruct students in how to relate letters and sounds, how to break words into sounds, and how to blend sounds to form words." Also, "students apply their knowledge of phonics as they read words, sentences, and text" and "students apply what they learn about sounds and letters to their own writing" (p. 6).

Throughout this book, you will see how phonics and spelling develop through early reading and writing activities. Using these multilevel activities, you will be able to meet the needs of all children in your kindergarten class, regardless of their ability levels.

Hopefully, you will find the time daily to read to students, to read with students using predictable big books, and to provide opportunities for students to read or pretend read by themselves.

So that all children make progress in writing, we suggest that **you model how to write by writing a Morning Message at the beginning of each day and/or a journal entry at the end of the day. Besides writing *for* students, you can also write *with* students when they do shared writing and make predictable charts. These writing activities help students become ready to write by themselves, so you need to provide opportunities for them.**

Emergent readers learn about letters, sounds, and words when they read nursery rhymes and rhyming books and talk about rhyming words. Focus on letter names and sounds as you talk about the names of the children in your class and the familiar words you encounter during The Opening and shared reading with predictable books. By asking, "What do you notice?" when talking about letters, words, and sentences, you encourage all children to contribute, regardless of their ability levels. Finally, as you work with environmental print (cereals, restaurants, and names), you give all children opportunities to practice letters and reading even if they come from homes without books.

August/September

The first day of kindergarten is here—**the biggest day for the littlest students in elementary school!** Teachers scurry to put all of the pieces in place and decorate their rooms. Are the bulletin boards up? Are the centers in the right places? Books, beads, puzzles, and boxes need to be within reach. Meanwhile, parents scurry to get haircuts, physicals, school supplies, and new outfits for their kindergarten students as they get ready for school. Here come the students!

Kindergartners at all different literacy levels must sense that they are making progress if their eagerness and excitement are to sustain them through the hard work of learning how to read and write.

This chapter includes activities for the first 4–6 weeks of the school year that help develop critical concepts and strategies while simultaneously convincing **all** students that they can successfully learn about reading, writing, and phonics in kindergarten. Kindergarten teachers have successfully used these activities with students at all stages of development.

The Opening

The kindergarten day begins in different ways in different classrooms. Some teachers start the day in centers; others choose to open with the big group. **To follow the activities in this book, call students together at the front of the room and begin the day as a group. Use the following questions with students:**

- **"Who is here today?"**

- **"Is anyone absent?"**

- **"What day of the week is it?"**

- **"What is the month? The date? The year?"**

- **"How many days have we been in school? Can anyone count them? Let's make a mark for each day."**

Some teachers mark the days by adding one straw to a jar per day. Teachers allow students to bundle the straws in groups of ten with rubber bands as the days progress so that students learn to count by ones and tens and later bundle the tens together to form a hundreds group. In this way, students learn about ones, tens, and hundreds in real ways. Place your calendar near the big group so that students can look at it, talk about the days of the week and the date, and chart the weather for the day. Talk about any plans and special events for the day. Discuss what book will be read aloud, what students will do in centers, or what students will learn about the current theme.

All of these naming activities (day of the week, month of the year, weather words) are important because next month, you will begin to stretch out these words, call attention to the sound at the beginning of each word, and look at the letters that make those sounds.

How The Opening Is Multilevel

During The Opening, kindergarten students learn about the reading and writing of numbers and words. What each student learns depends on what he already knows. While some students are learning numbers and number words, others are learning about the letters and sounds at the beginnings of these words. Still others are learning how to read or spell the words that are discussed and written on the board or written on word cards and placed in a pocket chart. The same is true for the days of the week, the months, weather words, and the current theme. In kindergarten, learning about reading and writing is done in an integrated way, and you can teach this during The Opening.

Reading Aloud to Students

Students love books and stories. Kindergarten teachers have always recognized the importance of reading a variety of books to their students. **Reading to students promotes oral language and concept development, adds to each student's store of information about the world, and helps students develop a sense of story.** Research tells us that students who come to schools ready to read come from homes where they have been read to (*Beginning to Read: Thinking and Learning about Print* by Marilyn Jager Adams, MIT Press, 1990).

Students who have been read to frequently before coming to school have increased syntactic and vocabulary development, increased desire and motivation to learn how to read, and more-developed concepts of print, according to Leslie Morrow and Linda Gambrell ("Literature Based Reading Instruction" in M. L. Kamil, P. B. Mosenthal, P. D. Pearson, and R. Barr, Eds. *Handbook of Reading Research,* Vol. III, pp. 563–586, 2000).

Your local or school library is filled with children's books, some of which have been children's favorites for years. These are the books to share with students. For example, as a kindergarten student, you may have listened to a teacher read *Curious George* books. Students still enjoy hearing how George's curiosity gets him into trouble. They also learn the meaning of the word *curious*.

Students need to hear both stories (fiction) and informational books (nonfiction). Some students like stories, while others prefer to learn more about the world. Books can take students as far away as Africa in *A Is for Africa* by Ifeoma Onyefulu (Puffin, 1997) or as near as a zoo or farm.

Read-aloud books should also include alphabet and rhyming books. Alphabet books focus students' attention on letters and sounds. Rhyming books help students understand rhyme. Both types of books help students develop phonemic awareness.

Reading aloud is important to students for learning meaning vocabulary. According to *Put Reading First*, "Children learn word meanings from listening to adults read to them. Reading aloud is particularly helpful when the reader pauses during reading to define an unfamiliar word and, after reading, engages the child in a conversation about the book. Conversations about books help children learn new words and concepts and to relate them to prior knowledge and experience" (p. 35).

August/September

Just as parents sit close to their children while reading to them, so should teachers. Sitting close to the teacher and the book helps students focus. If students are not used to having books read to them, you may have to talk to them about being good listeners. Kindergartners need to be told that the rules at school are different from those at home. Students will need to listen first, then ask questions. **Students at all levels can learn from listening to, talking about, and thinking about different kinds of books.**

When children have been read to since infancy, any book read to them is a treat. Easy books are always old favorites for them to listen to, and these children often have the attention span for longer books. For kindergarten students who have not had these literacy experiences, books with not much text (just a line or two on each page) will keep their attention. Many young children are attracted to the sound of language first. If books are written in rhyme, their ears seem to listen as their eyes watch the pictures and they see what the book is about. Some favorite books for kindergarten teachers to read at the beginning of the school year are the following:

Nonfiction

Amazing Airplanes by Tony Mitton and Ant Parker (Kingfisher, 2002)

Other books in this *Amazing Machines* series by Tony Mitton and Ant Parker include the following:

Busy Boats (Kingfisher, 2002)

Cool Cars (Kingfisher, 2002)

Dazzling Diggers (Kingfisher, 2000)

Flashing Fire Engines (Kingfisher, 2000)

Roaring Rockets (Kingfisher, 2000)

Terrific Trains (Kingfisher, 2000)

Tough Trucks (Kingfisher, 2005)

Tremendous Tractors (Kingfisher, 2005)

Country Fair by Gail Gibbons (Little, Brown and Company, 1994)

Alphabet Books

A Is for Animals: An ABC Pop-Up by David Pelham (Little Simon, 1991)

ABC I Like Me! by Nancy Carlson (Puffin, 1997)

All Aboard ABC by Douglas Magee and Robert Newman (Puffin, 1990)

Animal Parade by Jakki Wood (Scholastic, 1994)

David McPhail's Animals A to Z by David McPhail (Scholastic, 1989)

Miss Bindergarten Gets Ready for Kindergarten by Joseph Slate (Puffin, 2001)

Miss Bindergarten Stays Home from Kindergarten by Joseph Slate (Puffin, 2000)

The Night Before Kindergarten by Natasha Wing (Grosset & Dunlap, 2001)

Rhyming Books

Brown Bear, Brown Bear, What Do You See? by Bill Martin Jr. (Henry Holt and Company, 1967)

Five Little Monkeys Jumping on the Bed by Eileen Christelow (Clarion, 1989)

I Ain't Gonna Paint No More by Karen Beaumont (Harcourt Children's Books, 2005)

The Real Mother Goose (Rand McNally & Company, 1916)

Ten in the Bed by Jane Cabrera (Holiday House, 2006)

Fiction (Including Simple Stories and Familiar Songs)

Clifford the Big Red Dog by Norman Bridwell (Cartwheel, 1985)

The Complete Adventures of Curious George by Margret Rey and H. A. Rey (Houghton Mifflin, 1941)

Franklin Goes to School by Paulette Bourgeois (Scholastic, 1995)

If You're Happy and You Know It! by Jane Cabrera (Holiday House, 2005)

Kindergarten Kids by Ellen Sensi (Scholastic, 1994)

The Little Engine That Could by Watty Piper (Grosset & Dunlap, 1930)

Monster Goes to School by Virginia Mueller (Albert Whitman & Company, 1991)

My Brown Bear Barney by Dorothy Butler (Greenwillow Books, 1989)

Old MacDonald Had a Farm by Jane Cabrera (Holiday House, 2008)

School Bus by Donald Crews (HarperTrophy, 1987)

School Days by B. G. Hennessy (Puffin, 1990)

Timothy Goes to School by Rosemary Wells (Puffin, 1981)

The Very Hungry Caterpillar by Eric Carle (Penguin, 1987)

The Wheels on the Bus by Raffi (Crown Books for Young Readers, 1990)

Where the Wild Things Are by Maurice Sendak (HarperCollins, 1963)

Reading with Students

Shared Reading with Predictable Big Books

A child who was read to before beginning kindergarten usually sat on someone's lap or snuggled next to someone while being read to. Being read to in this way allowed him to look at the pictures and the print up close. He asked questions and talked about the book, often relating the book to his own life. He asked for the same book to be read over and over again, many times, until he had almost memorized the book. He knew whether the reader skipped a paragraph or page of his favorite book. He would stop the reader to say, "You forgot . . ." and turn back to the page so that the reader could read it correctly. The parents of this kind of child can often remember their child's favorite book even years later. For example, Michelle's favorite book as a three-year-old was *In a People House* by Dr. Seuss (Random House, 1972). Michelle is now a kindergarten teacher, and her parents can still recite the words from the book!

One particular kind of reading that is important for kindergartners is **shared reading with predictable big books. Predictable books are books with repeated patterns, refrains, pictures, and rhymes. Shared reading of predictable big books is an extension of the lap experience that children had at home.** Students can see both the pictures and the print as the teacher reads the book. And, just like at home, one reading is never enough! After two or three readings, some students naturally chime in, having memorized many of the words!

Reading requires particular ways of moving the eyes and an understanding of what letters, words, and sentences are. During shared reading of big books, focus on the print on the page and teach print concepts. Call attention to the front of the book or the cover as you read with students, point as you start on the left, go to the right, and make a return sweep to the next line. Match your words to the print: point to each word as you read it. Point to words as you talk about them. Point to certain letters—the first letter or last letter of a word and words that begin with the same letter on the same page—as you talk about them.

When choosing a big book for shared reading, consider the following:

1. The book must be predictable with repetitive sentence patterns, pictures to support the sentence patterns, and not too much print.

2. The book should be enjoyable and appealing to most students, since the entire class will work with the same big book.

3. The book must be able to take students somewhere conceptually. Most teachers spend a week or two with a book—reading, rereading, acting out the story, and building connections to themes and units to extend students' knowledge.

The repeated patterns, refrains, pictures, and rhymes in predictable books allow students to pretend read a book that has been read to them several times. **Pretend reading is a stage that most**

students go through with a favorite book that has been read and reread to them. Shared reading of predictable books allows all students to experience pretend reading.

To illustrate the many types of activities that you might do with a predictable big book, some examples with *From Head to Toe* by Eric Carle (HarperTrophy, 2007) are included. In this big book, each animal says something that it can do. Then, each animal asks the same question of the children, "Can you do it?" The penguin starts, "I am a penguin and I turn my head." Then, the penguin asks, "Can you do it?" A different child answers each question, but the answer is always the same: "I can do it!" The book ends with a child saying, "I am I and I wiggle my toe. Can you do it?" For this last question, a parrot answers the child, "I can do it! I can do it!"

> The most important goals for shared reading are that even students with no literacy backgrounds can pretend read the book after it has been read to them several times and that they develop the confidence that goes along with that accomplishment.

Before Reading

Talk about the cover: the title of the book, the author, and the picture(s). Then, have students locate those items on the cover. Next, take a picture walk through the book. Talk about the animals and what they are doing in the story. The names of the animals (penguin, giraffe, buffalo, monkey, seal, gorilla, cat, crocodile, camel, donkey, elephant), the body parts (head, neck, shoulders, arms, hands, chest, back, hips, knees, leg, foot, toe), and the actions (turn, bend, raise, wave, clap, thump, arch, wriggle, bend, kick, stomp, wiggle) are important words and may be new vocabulary for some children. When taking a picture walk, be sure to mention what animal is on each page and what is happening. If students don't know or can't tell from the picture, ask, "Do you think that the penguin is turning her head?" "Is the giraffe bending his neck?" Using the correct words for the animals, actions, and body parts is important when looking at the pictures so that children learn the vocabulary and understand each action.

During Reading

First, read the book to the class.

As with any book, the first and second readings should be strictly focused on the meaning and enjoyment of the book. *From Head to Toe* has delightful illustrations, and students enjoy seeing if they can do each action that the animals can do.

Then, encourage students to **join in the reading**; this is called **shared reading**. There are a variety of ways to encourage students to join in the reading. For this book, students will want to say the repeated response. "I can do it!" After the first reading, students can chime in every time a character in the book says "I can do it!" Read the first page and do the action. Then, let students read the next page and copy the action. Teach them how to whisper read if they yell rather than talk. Remember, this is called shared reading. It is important that all children try to read each page! Some will be more successful than others because some, having done this at home already, are more ready for this activity. For those who know letter sounds but do not think that they can read, tell them that the letters will help them remember the animal names (**p** for penguin; **g** for giraffe; **b** for buffalo; **m** for monkey; **s** for seal; another **g**, this time for gorilla; **c** for cat; **cr** for crocodile; **c** for camel; **d** for donkey; and **e** for elephant). Some letters and sounds are harder than others, especially the two **g**'s with two different sounds at the beginnings of **giraffe** and **gorilla**. The illustrations on each page will help with **g** and the three **c**'s for **cat**, **crocodile**, and **camel**. Once children know letter sounds, show them how this knowledge will help them when they are reading! For those who are not readers and haven't yet mastered the letter names and sounds, show them how the pictures can help. Three groups of learners can find success in different ways during this multilevel lesson.

After Reading

After reading, work on comprehension. One way to do this is by acting out the story. Young children are natural actors. They pretend and act out all kinds of things. Children do not need props or costumes to act out this story, but you may want to draw simple animal shapes on card stock or poster board, laminate the paper, punch two holes at the top of each, and tie lengths of yarn through the holes. Students can hang the cards around their necks, and everyone will know what characters they are. Act out the story once or twice so that each student has a chance to be one of the animals or so that some children can be the animals and some children can respond to the animals. When "doing" the book, you can read the parts that are not repetitive and let the children who have animal cards act them out, or you can have students say or read their parts. It depends on your students and how much help they need.

Make the Book Available

Make the big-book or little-book version available for students to read. Some teachers like to practice reading the story a few times with the class and record the story for the listening center. In the recording, the teacher reads the animals' answers and the class or small groups of students chime in for the repeated phrases. **Students delight in going to the listening center and listening to someone they know reading the book!** Some students will just listen to the story, turning each page at the right time. Other students will read the words along with the voices. Still other students may match the voices with the print on each page and really read.

How Shared Reading with Predictable Big Books Is Multilevel

During shared reading with a predictable big book, there are many things to notice. Students who come to kindergarten already beginning to read move further along in their reading because they learn more words and begin to notice similarities and differences in words. Students who come to kindergarten with little print experience learn what reading is and begin to develop concepts of print. Others begin to learn a few words and notice how words are the same and different. Most importantly, **all students develop the desire to learn how to read and the confidence that they are learning how to read!**

Favorite Big Books for August/September

Five Little Monkeys Jumping on the Bed by Eileen Christelow (Clarion, 1989)

The Gingerbread Man by Brenda Parkes and Judith Smith (Mimosa Publications, 2001)

Goldilocks and the Three Bears by David McPhail (Cartwheel, 1995)

The Little Red Hen by Paul Galdone (Clarion, 1973)

Rosie's Walk by Pat Hutchins (Aladdin, 1968)

Sheep on a Ship by Nancy Shaw (Houghton Mifflin, 1989)

Writing for Students

Morning Message

Morning Message is one way to write *for* students. So many things happen each day in school that kindergarten students often look forward to what will take place. It is a good idea to write a Morning Message each day. This Morning Message is written on a large piece of lined chart paper with a thick black marker. Many teachers do this at the beginning of the day or any time they call together the big group. Each sentence of the Morning Message should be written on a separate line until students have a good concept of what a sentence is. Then, begin to wrap the sentences around.

August/September

The first Morning Messages are simple and include just a sentence or two each, like the following:

> Dear Class,
>
> Today is Monday.
>
> We will learn a new song.
>
> Love,
>
> Mrs. Hall

Each day as you write, let students know what you are writing and why you are writing. In the first few messages, you will do all of the work while students listen and learn what to do and why.

"I will write a Morning Message. I will say and spell the words as I write. **Dear** capital D–e–a–r, **Class** capital C–l–a–s–s." Point to the comma and say, "This is a **comma** and it means to pause."

"The first sentence I will write is '**Today is Monday**.' **Today** Capital T–o–d–a–y, **is** i–s, **Monday** capital M–o–n–d–a–y." Write a period and point to it while saying, "This is a period. You put a period at the end of a sentence."

"Now, I will write the second sentence, '**We will learn a new song**.' **We** capital W–e, **will** w–i–l–l, **learn** l–e–a–r–n, **a**, **new** n–e–w, **song** s–o–n–g. I put a period at the end of this sentence." Point to the period as you say **period**.

"At the end of my message, I write the closing. I like to say, '**Love**.' Capital L–o–v–e, comma." Point to the comma you have just written and say, "Pause."

"I end the message with my name so that you will know that I wrote you this message. **Mrs.** capital M–r–s., **Hall** capital H–a–l–l."

"That is my Morning Message to you. It tells you what day it is and what we will do today."

"Let's look at the first sentence." Point to the first sentence. "How many words are in the first sentence?"

"Let's count the words in the first sentence and see." Encourage students to join in counting the words. Next, write the numeral three after the sentence with a colorful marker.

"Let's count the words in the second sentence." Point to the second sentence and count. Write the numeral six after the second sentence with the same marker.

"Which sentence has more words?" Call on a student who raises his hand. "Right, the second sentence has more words—it has six words."

"Let's count the letters in the first sentence: one, two, three, four, five, six, seven, eight, nine, ten, eleven, twelve, thirteen. There are thirteen letters in the first sentence."

16 © Carson-Dellosa · · · · · · CD-104274 · **Month-by-Month Reading, Writing, and Phonics for Kindergarten**

"Let's count the letters in the second sentence: one, two, three, four, five, six, seven, eight, nine, ten, eleven, twelve, thirteen, fourteen, fifteen, sixteen, seventeen, eighteen, nineteen. There are nineteen letters in the second sentence."

"Which sentence has more letters?" Call on a student who raises her hand. "You are right. The second sentence has more words and more letters."

"What do you notice about the Morning Message?" This is the time to let students tell you if any words rhyme or begin like their name, with capital letters, or with the same letter sounds, etc. If you want students to notice something, this is also the time to point it out.

When writing the Morning Message during the first month of school, concentrate on saying the words and saying each letter as you write it. Kindergarten students are not expected to learn to spell these words, but many will learn the letter names and will be able to recognize letters because they listen to you say the letters as you write them. Early in the school year, concentrate on the following:

- Writing what you say
- Showing where to start writing and which way to go (left to right)
- Showing where to begin the next sentence or line (top to bottom)
- Saying the words, then saying each letter one at a time as it is written
- Using capital letters
- Using punctuation
- Counting sentences
- Counting words in sentences
- Counting letters in sentences
- Finding out which sentence has more words/letters
- Clapping the syllables in words (to-day, is, Mon-day)
- Talking about how to start and end a message ("Who remembers how I start/end my message each day?")
- Talking about things that happen each day
- Talking about special events that happen to your students

See the Morning Message chart in *Building Blocks "Plus" for Kindergarten Bulletin Board* (Carson-Dellosa, 1998) to begin.

Some appropriate topics for Morning Messages during the first month of school are the following:

- Writing about the day of the week and the date (Today is Tuesday. It is September 5, 2009.)
- Writing about the weather (Today is Wednesday. It is raining.)
- Writing the names of special students (Today is Thursday. Erica is our special student.)

- Writing about students' birthdays (Today is Friday. It is Jacob's birthday.)

- Writing about someone who will visit the classroom (Today is Tuesday. Our principal, Mrs. Smith, will visit today.)

- Writing about something that the class will do that day (Today is Monday. We will go to music.)

- Writing about a nursery rhyme, fingerplay, or song that the class will learn (Today is Wednesday. We will learn "Humpty Dumpty.")

How Writing for Students Is Multilevel

When you write for students who are beginning their literacy journeys, they learn what writing is, why we write, and how we write. Some students learn the letter names as you say each letter and write it. For those students who are further along in their literacy journeys, writing for students is important too. When you think, write, and talk about what you will say and how you will write those thoughts, you are modeling many skills (sentence structure, capitalization, punctuation, etc.) that are appropriate for the more-advanced students. The open-ended questions you ask after completing the writing ("What do you notice about this message?") lead students to notice different things depending on their literacy levels. What you talk about and how much you interact with students changes over the months as students do more of the work and writing becomes interactive.

Writing with Students

Predictable Charts

Structured Language Experience is what Pat Cunningham once called Predictable Charts (For more information on Predictable Charts, see *Predictable Charts* by Dorothy Hall and Elaine Williams (Carson-Dellosa, 2002). If a teacher chooses a predictable pattern, begins a sentence with that pattern, and calls on students to dictate sentences using the same pattern, all students can take part in this task. It is based on this language experience:

1. The teacher writes what the child says.

2. The child can read what the teacher writes.

One of the easiest predictable charts to begin with is "My name is . . . ." Start the year by doing some get-acquainted activities and learning students' names. Write *Names* on the top of the chart. The first sentence you write is "My name is **Mrs. Hall**." Then, call on the student of the day to tell what his name is. Michael says, "My name is **Michael**." Write the words as Michael says them. Next, call on another student, who answers, "My name is **Jasmine**." One by one, each child uses this model and completes the sentence with her name.

Days 1–2: Dictation of the Sentences

After talking about students' names, begin your predictable chart with the sentence "My name is . . . ." Model by completing the first sentence. After writing your sentence, read it to the class, pointing to each word as you say it. Then, ask students, "Who wants to do the next sentence?" Have the student you call on say, "My name is . . ." and complete the sentence with his name. As each child dictates a sentence, write it on the chart. Completing the chart will take one day if you have 10–12 students or two days if you have a larger class. If some students need extra help, do not call on them for the first sentences so that they have time to see examples. After a few sentences, students pick up the pattern and can be successful.

The finished chart might look like this:

```
        Names

My name is Mrs. Hall.

My name is Michael.

My name is Jasmine.

My name is Erica.

My name is Mike.

My name is Ryan.

My name is Refugio.

My name is Christopher.

My name is Benjamin.

My name is Nikki.

My name is Tiara.

My name is Ed.

My name is Mitchell.

My name is Julie.

My name is Carlos.

My name is Rashawn.

My name is Renee.

My name is Suzanne.

My name is Michelle.
```

Day 3: Touch Reading the Sentences

On the third day, ask each student to touch read her sentence on the chart. The student reads, "My name is . . ." and says her name, touching each word on the chart as she reads it. Start at the top of the chart and read to the bottom.

Day 4: Sentence Builders

Today, focus on the sentence, words, sounds of letters, and letters. Before the lesson, write three sentences from the chart on separate sentence strips. The name of the child who dictated each sentence is included with the sentence. Cut apart the words and put them in an envelope or plastic bag. One sentence at a time, pass out the words to four students, making sure to give the name card to the child whose sentence you will build. Ask students to be sentence builders. To do this correctly, the child holding **My** stands at the beginning of the sentence. The next place in line belongs to the child holding **name**. In the third place is the child holding **is**. The last spot belongs to the child holding his name. Finally, read the sentence with the class. Stand behind each sentence-builder student and touch her shoulder as you read the word she is holding. Repeat this process for the other sentences.

Day 5: Making a Class Book

If you think that the class needs an easy task early in the year, have students make a class book. Write the predictable part of each sentence from the chart on the bottoms of large pieces of drawing paper. Then, let students add their names to the sentence "My name is . . . ." All students need to do is illustrate their sentences after they have written their names. To finish the book, make a front cover (with a title) and a back cover (plain) and staple the pages inside in the order in which they appear on the chart. Now, students have a class big book with the names of the students in their class. Making

a class book becomes a multilevel activity when students read it. Some students will be able to read each sentence, including the names of their classmates. Others will be able to read just the sentences containing their names. Still others pick up the book and search for the pages with their names because these are the first words they can read. This class big book, written by students and including all of their names and self-portraits, is a wonderful addition to any kindergarten classroom.

Other Ideas for Predictable Charts

Another Predictable Chart to make early in the year, especially when studying colors, is My Favorite Color. Students use the predictable pattern "I like . . ." and name their favorite colors. For this chart, write who said each sentence in parentheses after the sentence. Here is an example:

```
          My Favorite Color

    I like green. (Colby)

    I like red. (Kendra)

    I like blue. (Audrey)

    I like purple. (Thomas)
```

You can also take a trip around the school and write a chart about what the class sees. Title the chart *Our Trip around the School*. The predictable sentence starter would be "I saw . . ." (children, classes, the cafeteria, the gym, the office, the nurse's office, the music room, etc.).

How Writing a Predictable Chart Is Multilevel

Cutting sentences into words, rearranging them, and having students put the words in the right order and make new sentences from familiar word patterns helps students understand what words are. When writing a predictable chart, there are many things for students to notice. Students with little print experience learn what reading is and begin to develop print concepts. They learn that each sentence starts at the left and goes to the right. They see you start at the top of the page and go to the bottom. They hear you talk about letters, words, and sentences and learn about these things. Students who come to kindergarten already reading can usually read the whole chart and further their reading skills as they learn more words and see the similarities and differences between them.

Writing by Students

At the beginning of the year, it is a good idea to get a baseline of where your kindergartners are in their writing abilities before phonics instruction begins. Some children come to kindergarten reading, but many are not able to write much except for their names. One way to get young children to write is to model the different ways that people write, give each child a plain piece of paper, and ask students to write for you.

Tell the class that some people use pictures when they write. Draw a smiling face on the board to illustrate this:

"When you see this face, you know that someone is happy or likes what she is doing. If someone wrote I, then drew a smiling face and a piece of pizza, what would she be saying?"

I

"Yes, she would be saying that she likes pizza!"

Next, draw some wavy lines.

"Some people pretend to write when they do not know how to write or which letters to make. I did this when I was little, and I thought that I was writing like my family did. When you write, it is OK to pretend to write."

Then, write a few words that students might know:

cat

love

Miss Williams

"Some people use words that they know to write messages. You know that this says **cat**, this says **love**, and this is my name, **Miss Williams**."

August/September $\cdots\cdots\cdots\cdots\cdots\cdots\cdots\cdots\cdots\cdots\cdots\cdots\cdots$

Write a few simple sentences on the board:

I love you.

I love my cat.

While you are writing, say something like the following:

> "Some of you may be able to use words and sentences when writing—just like I do. Sometimes, we are not sure what letters are in the words that we want to write, so we stretch out the words, listen for the sounds, and write the letters that make those sounds."

Stretch out some of the words you have written on the board so that students can see you write each letter as they hear the sound (l–o–v–e, c–a–t, p–i–z–z–a).

These are some examples of children's writing during the first weeks of kindergarten:

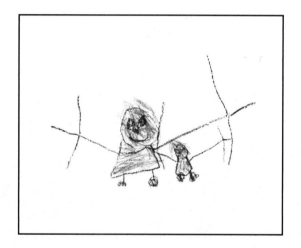 

Getting to Know You

Developing Phonemic Awareness and Learning Letters and Sounds

Most kindergarten teachers begin the year with get-acquainted activities. As a part of these activities, teachers often focus on a special student each day. In addition to learning about each classmate, students can focus attention on the special student's name and use the name to develop some important understandings about words and letters.

To prepare for this activity, write all students' first names (with initials for last names if two names are the same) with a thick black marker on sentence strips. Cut the strips so that long names have long strips and short names have short strips. Place the strips in a box. Each day, reach into the box and draw a name. This child becomes the special student for the day, and his name becomes the focus of many activities. Reserve space on a wall or a bulletin board and add each child's name to the wall as it is selected. Some teachers take pictures of students or have students bring in snapshots of themselves to add to the wall as names are added. Other teachers gather student drawings of each special student and put together a class book at the end of the activity. The teacher titles this book *Our Class* and places it in the reading center for students to enjoy.

Some activities that you might do with students' names are the following:

First Name/Day

Close your eyes. Reach into the box, shuffle the names, and draw one. Call that student to the front of the room and name her special student for the day! Lead the class in interviewing this child. Find out what she likes to eat, play, do after school, etc. Does she have brothers? Sisters? Cats? Dogs? Focus attention on the student's name—**Jasmine**. Point to **Jasmine** on the sentence strip and develop students' understanding of jargon by pointing out that this **word** is Jasmine's name. Tell students that it takes many **letters** to write **Jasmine** and let them help you count the letters. Say **J–a–s–m–i–n–e** and have students chant the letters with you. Point out that Jasmine **begins** with the letter **J**. Explain that the **J** looks bigger than the other letters because it is a **capital J**, and the other letters are **small** letters (or **uppercase/lowercase**—whatever jargon you use).

Let Jasmine lead the class in a cheer with the letters in her name. "Give me a **J**." Students shout, "**J**." "Give me an **a**. Give me an **s**. Give me an **m**. Give me an **i**. Give me an **n**," and finally, "Give me an **e**. What do you have?" "**Jasmine**." "What do you have?" "**Jasmine**." "Yeah!"

Another activity that helps students develop phonemic awareness is clapping the syllables in words. This helps students develop the ability to segment words into sounds and syllables. Pick a name and say the name, clapping the syllables of the name as you say it. Say the name again, having students clap with you. The term **syllables** may be difficult for students to understand, so you may want to refer to syllables as **beats**. By clapping, students should realize that **Mike** is a one-beat word, **Jasmine** is a two-beat word, and **Refugio** is a four-beat word.

This month, identify other things in the room that begin like the names of students you spotlight in Getting to Know You. For **Rashawn**, you might mention Ryan's or Robert's name. Then, say, "I see some things in our classroom that begin with the same sound. What about the r–r–rocking chair? R–r–r–ocking chair begins like **Rashawn**. Do you see any more?" Help students recognize and name the things in your classroom that begin with **r**—rug, radio, rainbow, rooster, etc.

If there are letters and sounds that are not covered with students' names, you may want to discuss those letters and the sounds they make. For example, if you had one name that began with **n** (**Nikki**), you might want to talk about the other names that are not under the letter **n** but that contain an **n**, like: Jasmine, Suzanne, Ryan, and Rashawn. Stretch out each name and listen for the **n** sound. Ask students where they hear the **n** after each name is said. If you think that students need practice with a letter (for example, the only **f** in the names may be an **f** in the middle of **Refugio**), then use *Making Alphabet Books to Teach Letters and Sounds* (Hall, Carson-Dellosa, 2002) to go over some of the letters with which students need additional practice. Some teachers review all of the letters and their sounds with *Making Alphabet Books* in case some students would benefit from the additional practice.

Have students watch as you write **Jasmine** on a sentence strip. Have them chant the letters with you. Cut apart the word and mix up the letters. Let Jasmine arrange the letters in order so that they spell her name. Have other students chant to check the order. Shuffle the letters and let another student arrange the letters in order.

Give each child a large sheet of drawing paper and let students use crayons to write **Jasmine** in large letters on one side. On the board, model how to write each letter as students write. Do not worry if students' writing is not perfect or bears little resemblance to what you wrote. Resist the temptation to correct what students write. Remember that students who write at home before coming to school often reverse letters and write them in funny ways.

> The important concepts for students to understand is that names are words, that words can be written, and that it takes a lot of letters to write words.

Finally, have everyone look at Jasmine and talk about what she is wearing. Then, let students draw pictures of Jasmine on the other sides of their drawing papers. Save the drawing Jasmine did of herself with her name printed on the back. Post Jasmine's name strip on the wall along with her drawing (and/or photograph). Let Jasmine take home all of the other drawings!

Second Name/Day

Draw another name—**Ryan**. Whatever interviewing you did for Jasmine, do for Ryan. **(Decide carefully what you will do for the first child because every child will expect equal treatment!)**

Focus students' attention on Ryan's name. Say the letters in **Ryan**. Have students chant them with you. Help students count the letters and decide which letter is first, last, etc. Let Ryan lead the class in cheering and clapping his name. Write **Ryan** on another sentence strip and cut it into letters. Have Ryan arrange the letters to spell his name. Then, let him choose another child to do the same. Students can use the first sentence strip name (Jasmine) as a model.

Put Ryan's name on the wall under Jasmine's name and compare them. Which name has more letters? How many more letters are in **Jasmine** than in **Ryan**? Does **Ryan** have any of the same letters as **Jasmine**?

Finish the lesson by having everyone write **Ryan**. Have students look at Ryan and what he is wearing. Then, ask them to draw Ryan's picture. Let Ryan take home all of the drawings except for the drawing he did of himself, which will be posted on the wall and may later become his page in the class book. (More information about class books can be found on pages 20 and 38.)

Third Name/Day

Draw the third name—**Michelle**. Interview Michelle and chant the letters in Michelle's name. Let Michelle lead the class in cheering the letters in her name and then clapping the parts of her name. Write her name on a sentence strip, cut it into letters, and have Michelle arrange the letters. Then, let her choose another student to do the same. Be sure to note the two **l**'s and two **e**'s and talk about first and last letters. Which is the capital letter, and where is the capital letter in Michelle's name?

As you put Michelle's name on the wall, compare it to Jasmine's and Ryan's names. This is a perfect time to notice that all names begin with capital letters but not always with the same letter. If two names begin with the same letter and the same sound, point that out. Finish the lesson by having students write **Michelle** and draw her picture, saving Michelle's drawing for the wall and class book.

Fourth Name/Day

David is chosen next. Do all of the usual activities. When you put David's name on the wall, help students realize that Ryan still has the shortest name. (Ed may now look at the name card on his desk and call out that his name is even shorter. Point out that he is right but that Ryan's name is the shortest name on the wall now.) What is fascinating about this activity is how students compare their names to those on the wall even before their names are chosen. **This is exactly the kind of word/letter awareness you are trying to develop!**

Fifth Name/Day

Mike is drawn next. Do all of the usual activities. Then, take advantage of the fact that many words rhyme with **Mike**. Pair words with **Mike**. Say some words that rhyme with **Mike** and some that do not: Mike/bike, Mike/hat, Mike/hike, Mike/boy, Mike/pike, Mike/Mary, etc. If a word rhymes with **Mike**, students should point to Mike and shout, "Mike." If a word does not rhyme, students should shake their heads and frown. This develops the phonemic awareness concept of rhyme.

Each day, continue drawing a name, interviewing the student, letting the student lead her name cheer, clapping the syllables in her name, listening for the sounds the letters make, comparing the name and letter sounds to the other names on the wall, etc.

How Getting to Know You Is Multilevel

Getting to Know You is truly a multilevel activity. All students learn the names of their classmates and learn something about themselves on the day when they are spotlighted. Students learn how to read and write many names, and as they focus on which names have which letters, they learn letter names. Students begin to associate letters and sounds with the names they are learning, and they begin to learn print concepts and jargon.

Developing Phonemic Awareness and Phonics: Names

As students listen to the sounds they hear in Getting to Know You and look at the letters in each name, they are developing phonemic awareness. When students compare names and learn that **Michelle**, **Mike**, and **Monica** all have the same sound at the beginnings and all begin with the same letter, they begin to isolate sounds, or phonemes, and make connections between these sounds and letter names. They are learning phonics!

Developing Phonemic Awareness

Nursery Rhymes

The ability to recite nursery rhymes is considered an indicator of phonemic awareness. **Phonemic awareness develops through a series of stages** during which students become aware that language is made up of individual **words**, that words are made up of **syllables**, and that syllables are made up of **phonemes**. It is important to note that students do not learn this jargon. Five-year-olds cannot tell you there are three syllables in **dinosaur** and one syllable in **bat**. What they can do is clap the three beats in **dinosaur** and the one beat in **bat**. Likewise, they cannot tell you that the first phoneme in **bat** is **b**, but they can tell you that if you took **b** off of **bat**, you would have **at**.

> One of the best indicators of how well students will learn how to read is their ability to recite nursery rhymes when they walk into kindergarten.

Students develop this phonemic awareness as a result of the oral and written language to which they are exposed. Nursery rhymes, chants, and Dr. Seuss books usually play a large role in this development. This month, **read and share a lot of nursery rhymes with students**. Students should learn to recite, sing, clap, and pantomime the nursery rhymes. Some classes develop raps for the rhymes.

Once students can recite a lot of nursery rhymes, the nursery rhymes can be used to teach the concept of **rhyme**. Divide the class into two groups. One half of the class says the nursery rhyme but stops when they get to the rhyming word. The other half of the class waits to shout the rhyming word at the appropriate moment:

Jack and Jill

First Half: "Jack and Jill went up the . . ."

Second Half: "hill"

First Half: "To fetch a pail of water.

                 Jack fell down,

                 And broke his . . ."

Second Half: "crown;"

First Half: "And Jill came tumbling after."

Humpty Dumpty

First Half: "Humpty Dumpty sat on a wall.

                 Humpty Dumpty had a great . . ."

Second Half: "fall."

First Half: "All the king's horses,
                 And all the king's men,
                 Couldn't put Humpty
                 together . . . "

Second Half: "again."

Students also enjoy making familiar rhymes silly by adding a new word that rhymes. For example:

   Jack be nimble.

   Jack be quick.

   Jack jump over Pat and Rick!

Nursery rhymes have been a part of our oral heritage for generations. **It is now known that the rhythms and rhymes inherent in nursery rhymes are important vehicles for the beginning development of phonemic awareness.** Nursery rhymes should play a large role in any kindergarten curriculum.

How Nursery Rhymes Are Multilevel

Nursery rhymes are as multilevel as what the teacher does with them. First, chant the nursery rhymes with students so that they can say and hear the rhymes. Once students can recite the rhymes, show them the rhymes in a big book or written on a chart so that they see the print. Making nursery rhyme books using students' favorite rhymes gives students opportunities to try to match pictures, rhymes, and print. Some students see the pictures and remember the rhymes, other students pretend read the rhymes, and still others really read the rhymes by placing their fingers under each word while reading it and cross-checking with the letter sounds they know. You can also say three words: two that are the same and one that is different. Have students tell you the two words that are the same and the one that is different. For example, you could say **Jack, Jack, Jill; Jill, Humpty, Humpty; king, men, king; wall, wall, fall;** etc. What a child does with pictures and print depends on what she knows and where she is in her literacy development.

Centers

Kindergarten classrooms are famous for centers—the Play or Dress-Up Center, Kitchen Center, Art Center, Writing Center, Reading Center, Science Center, etc. **Learning Centers are an important part of a developmental kindergarten. It is in these centers that students explore and discover their environment individually or in small groups.** This book focuses on centers where students practice reading, writing, and working with words—the Reading Center and the Writing Center. For more information on these centers and activities in all centers, see *Learning Centers in Kindergarten* by Karen Loman and Dorothy Hall (Carson-Dellosa, 2004).

Reading Center

The Reading Center should be a pleasant, cozy place. Some teachers use furniture that has been donated to the classroom for the Reading Center. Some schools buy child-size chairs and sofas, and other schools build reading lofts.

Important things to remember about the Reading Center:

1. Students should have a comfortable place to read alone or with a friend.

2. There should be a lot of good books and other reading materials from which to choose.

Books that the teacher has read to the class are always favorites for the Reading Center, whether they are big books or little books. Books that contain stories that students have heard many times and books that were read to students before they entered kindergarten should also be included. Informational books and magazines should be available in the Reading Center. As the school year progresses, class books and student-authored books can be added to the Reading Center.

Include favorite stories, books that you are reading to students daily, fiction and nonfiction rhyming books (including nursery rhymes), alphabet books, big books, and books you are reading during shared reading.

Writing Center

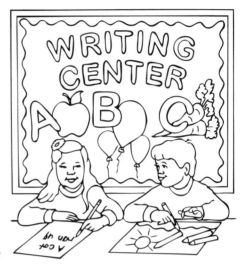

A variety of writing materials (pencils, pens, markers, crayons, etc.) and different kinds of paper (construction, newsprint, lined and unlined paper, etc.) should be available in the Writing Center. As students begin kindergarten, they should be encouraged to copy text from the boards and charts in the classroom: their own names, other students' names, color words, and number words. Also, they should be told that it is OK to draw, pretend write, or "drite" (a combination of drawing and writing) in the Writing Center. Students who have written at home will have no problem doing this. Some students may feel that they need permission to scribble or write the best that they can. They get that permission when they see you model this or praise and display the work of students making their first attempts at writing. Most kindergarten students enjoy having envelopes in the center too. This way, they can deliver their messages to family members or friends and feel grown-up. You may need to make rules for students—each student should use no more than one envelope each time he visits the Writing Center!

How Reading and Writing Centers Are Multilevel

When students work in centers, they have opportunities to learn through play. Some students get their first chances to hold books and turn the pages in the Reading Center. This activity is an important part of learning how to read. Some students pretend read and show the pictures to an invisible audience, especially if this is the only way they have ever seen someone (a teacher) reading!

Other students look for their favorite books or books on a topic about which they want to learn more (even if they are just reading the pictures). Still other students really read books or try to match the print in the book to the letters and sounds that they already know.

Some students have their first opportunities to write in the Writing Center because the writing instruments used in kindergarten (pencils, pens, markers, crayons, etc.) have not been available in their homes. Others need time to scribble and to pretend write. Finally, students who know what writing is and why we write have opportunities to write for real reasons (messages, lists, etc.). Reading and Writing Centers are multilevel by nature because students explore these special places on their own.

October

October is a busy month in kindergarten! Many students are still learning about each other during Getting to Know You activities. They are learning more about their school by talking about special people in the school (principal, art teacher, etc.). Fall is a great time to learn about colors! Pumpkins appear in many classrooms, pumpkin patches, and stores. Autumn is here!

The Opening

- **"Who is here today?"**
- **"Is anyone absent?"**
- **"What day of the week is it?"**
- **"What is the month? The date? The year?"**
- **"How many days have we been in school? Can anyone count them? Let's make a mark for each day."**

Add a straw to the jar. The straws are grouped in bundles of ten, and students count along with you. They count tens and ones to find out how many days they have been in school. The calendar for October is posted on a bulletin board where students can see it. Talk about the day of the week, the date, and chart the weather each day this month.

As the calendar becomes more familiar, draw attention to the beginnings of words. In particular, ask students to stretch out words and help them notice the beginnings of words on the calendar and bulletin board by asking questions such as the following:

- **"How do you know that this says Monday?"**
- **"Can you find the word Monday on the calendar? What do you notice about Monday?"**

The answers vary depending on which students you ask. Some answers include these:

"It starts with **M**."

"**Monday** starts like **Michelle** or **Mom**."

Then, ask, "Who can point to **M** in **Monday**? What day comes before **Monday**? What day comes after **Monday**? What do we usually do on **Monday** that is special?"

Next, talk about the weather.

"Today is sunny. Stretch out the word **sunny**. Who can find a word on the bulletin board that starts with that sound? Yes, **sunny** starts with that sound and begins with **s**."

Tell students something that happened to you yesterday or let some students share their experiences. Talk about special days. If the class will attend a special session or class (art, music, media center, etc.), talk about it. Many teachers also share favorite books on the current theme.

Reading Aloud to Students

Kindergarten teachers need to read to students at least once every day. It is OK to read a book to students just for the pleasure of hearing a good story. As you are reading, students are developing important language skills. Students need to learn how to listen, think about the story and sequence of events, try to predict what might happen, and take turns answering questions about the story. While listening to the teacher read, kindergartners hear the sounds of letters and the sounds in words.

After reading a book aloud to students, ask, "How would you read this book if you picked it up? Could you read all of the words?" Remind students that most kindergartners can't! "Could you read the pictures? Could you retell the story?" Talk about the best way to pretend read each book that you read to the class this month.

Young students like to learn about new people and places. When you read informational books to the class, students have opportunities to learn while listening. Placing the books you read in the Reading Center gives students a chance to visit the book again and again.

Favorite Books for October

Colors

Brown Bear, Brown Bear, What Do You See? by Bill Martin Jr. (Henry Holt and Company, 1967)

Color Dance by Ann Jonas (Greenwillow Books, 1989)

Crabby Cat's Party by Joy Cowley (Dominie Press, 2004)

Frederick by Leo Lionni (Pantheon, 1967)

Freight Train by Donald Crews (Greenwillow Books, 1978)

Green Eggs and Ham by Dr. Seuss (Random House, 1960)

The Green Queen by Nick Sharratt (Candlewick, 1992)

Harold and the Purple Crayon by Crockett Johnson (HarperTrophy, 1955)

I Went Walking by Sue Williams (Harcourt Brace, 1989)

The Little Red Hen by Lucinda McQueen (Scholastic, 1985)

Polar Bear, Polar Bear, What Do You Hear? by Bill Martin Jr. (Puffin, 1991)

White Is the Moon by Valerie Greeley (Atheneum, 1991)

White Rabbit's Color Book by Alan Baker (Kingfisher Books, 1994)

Who Said Red? by Mary Serfozo (Aladdin Books, 1992)

October

Autumn

Halloween by Miriam Nerlove (Albert Whitman & Company, 1987)

Haunted House by Bill Martin Jr. (Harcourt, 1970)

How Do Apples Grow? by Betsy Maestro (HarperTrophy, 1993)

It's Pumpkin Time by Zoe Hall (Scholastic, 1994)

Johnny Appleseed by Steven Kellogg (Scholastic, 1989)

The Seasons of Arnold's Apple Tree by Gail Gibbons (Voyager, 1988)

Reading with Students

Shared Reading with Predictable Big Books

Brown Bear, Brown Bear, What Do You See? by Bill Martin Jr. (Henry Holt and Company, 1967) This is a favorite big book to read while students are learning about colors. It is a fun and easy way for students to learn about colors and color names as they enjoy the book's repetitive pattern, pictures, and print.

Before Reading

Take a picture walk through the book. Talk about the animals on each page and look for the name of the animal on the page. Call attention to the letter with which each animal's name begins and the sound at the beginning of the animal's name. Talk about the color of each animal and look for the color words on each page.

During Reading

The first reading of this big book is done by the teacher so that students can focus on the meaning and enjoyment of the story. The book has delightful illustrations. Students enjoy finding out which animal illustrates each color. As you read the book, call attention to each color and the animal pictured for it. Are all ducks yellow? Are all dogs white? Are all (or any) elephants pink? The predictable text makes it easy for kindergarten students to chime in—and they do!

During the next reading, encourage students to join in and share the reading. Once students have picked up the repetition in the questions and responses, students will want to join in the reading. You might read each question:

> "Brown Bear, Brown Bear, What do you see?"

Let students read each response:

> "I see a red bird looking at me."

Or, divide the class in half and let each half take turns reading the questions and responses.

After Reading

Focus on comprehension and discuss the animals and the color of each animal in this story. Next, work on sequence: "What animal did we meet first, second, next, etc." Another favorite after-reading activity in kindergarten is acting out the story.

Brown Bear, Brown Bear, What Do You See? is a natural story for acting out. Let each student be a character. Give craft-stick puppets or laminated, yarned picture-card necklaces to students to act out the parts.

This book calls for multiple days and multiple readings. Each day, read the story for a **different** purpose and do a **different** after-reading activity. Tell students what they will do after reading so that they will focus on this while reading the book. ("After reading, we will talk about all of the animals we met and what colors they are." "Today when we read, pay attention to the order we meet the animals. We will talk about this after we read the story.")

Crabby Cat's Party by Joy Cowley (Dominie Press, 2004)
This is another book that includes color words, and it can also be used to discuss emotions. (There are 12 themes in this series that are perfect for Shared reading in kindergarten and Crabby Cat is the star of many of the books.)

Before Reading

First, talk about the cover, the title, and the author. Show students the cover and ask them who they think Crabby Cat is. (Answer: The cat on the cover!) Then, take a picture walk through the book and have students discuss what they think is happening on each page. What is Crabby Cat doing in each picture? What other characters are in the book? How does Crabby look in the pictures at the beginning of the book? How does he look in the pictures at the end of the book? A cover talk and picture walk are always good before-reading activities for shared reading with big books.

During Reading

First, read the book to students, but don't stop there. Always read the book a second time the same day and invite the students to join in and share the reading of this book. You may still have to remind students to whisper read or read with little voices when it is their turn to help with the reading. Read the first page when Crabby Cat gets an invitation to a party and says, "I don't like parties!" Remind children that the pictures will help them remember all of the other things that Crabby Cat does not like. Then, let students read the following five pages on which Crabby puts on blue pants, green socks, and red shoes and says, "I don't like blue pants (and green socks and red shoes)." Next, let students read the pages on which Crabby Cat goes to the party and says, "I don't like purple balloons!" and "I don't like party hats!" Tell students that you will read the next two pages (pages 8–9). Then, let students help you read the "Happy Birthday to You" page. Many students will know and remember those words. Read, "I like blue pants." Then, let students complete the next four pages with "I like . . ." and "Happy Birthday to . . ." lyrics. If you have time, talk about the exclamation points at the ends of some sentences. Read the book again and make sure that students read those sentences in an exclamatory manner. Young children like to reread books because each book becomes more familiar and they get better at reading the book each time they do it.

After Reading

Ask some comprehension questions: "Who is this book about? Who are the other characters? Where does it take place? What happens in the beginning, in the middle, and at the end?" Do not ask only literal questions. Ask big questions, questions that will make students think: "How does Crabby Cat change at the birthday party? What causes him to change? What was your favorite part of this book?" You do not always have to act out the book after reading. You can also have students draw their favorite parts of the story as an after-reading activity.

Make the Books Available

Remember that students who are read to at home have their favorite books read to them over and over. Then, they pretend they can read them, and they often actually learn how to read them. Be sure to put favorite big books and/or little-book versions in the Reading Center for students to enjoy. Add to the fun by putting recordings of the stories and props in a Listening Center so that students can act out the stories!

Writing for Students

Morning Message

Continue to write the Morning Message for students.

Dear Class, Today is Tuesday, October 6, 2009. What will we read about today? Love, Mrs. Hall	Dear Class, Today is Wednesday, October 5, 2009. Yesterday, we read <u>Pumpkin Pumpkin</u>. Love, Mrs. Hall

After several weeks of writing Morning Messages and doing all of the work yourself, begin to ask students to use what they have learned to help you write this month:

- How do I start my Morning Message?
- Where do I start my Morning Message?
- What sound do you hear at the beginning of **Dear**?
- What letter do I write at the beginning of **Dear**?

- Do I begin **Dear** with a capital letter?

- What do I put at the end of a sentence? (Write some sentences that end with question marks and exclamation points as well as periods.)

- What do I put at the end of a question?

- How do I show that we are excited?

- How do I end my Morning Message?

- Can you help me spell **love**?

- What letter does **Mrs.** begin with? What does **Hall** begin with?

- Can you find a word you know and circle it? (Start to work on high-frequency words.)

- Can you find a word that begins like _____?

- Can you find a word that rhymes with _____?

Writing with Students

Predictable Charts

Just as kindergarten classes enjoy reading predictable books together, they also like to write and read predictable charts. Writing a predictable chart is a natural follow-up to reading a predictable book or introducing a topic/theme. A good predictable big book to use to begin writing predictable charts is *Things I Like* by Anthony Browne (Dragonfly Books, 1989). This is the story of a little chimp who tells about the things that he likes ("This is me and this is what I like: Painting . . . and riding my bike. Playing with toys, and dressing up."). **The pictures in the book make it predictable, not the pattern!**

After reading and enjoying the book, make a Things I Like chart. Put the title *Things I Like* on the top line of a large sheet of chart paper. As you write the title, say each word and each letter in each word so that students watch the left-to-right progression and the letter formation.

Next, write what you like to do, followed by your name in parentheses. This becomes a model for students to follow. Ask each child to tell something she likes or likes to do. Write students' answers on the predictable chart and place each child's name in parentheses after his sentence.

An example of a completed chart can be found on page 36.

....

This is what the completed chart might look like:

Things I Like

I like reading books. (Miss Williams)

I like swimming. (Madeline)

I like eating french fries. (Jasmine)

I like pizza. (Jeremis)

I like computers. (Ryan)

I like running. (Adam)

I like playing football. (Refugio)

I like riding my bike. (William)

I like playing basketball. (Erica)

I like making cookies. (Olivia)

I like going to the beach. (Mike)

I like making cookies. (Nikki)

I like watching TV. (Paul)

I like playing with my friends. (Mitchell)

I like soccer. (Jacob)

I like school. (Emma)

I like my dolls. (Ava)

I like going to the mall. (Rashawn)

I like my teacher. (Tiara)

I like reading books. (Lauren)

I like drawing pictures. (Christopher)

I like centers. (Paul)

I like playing outside. (Mitchell)

I like school! (Richard)

Touch Reading the Chart

On the following day, have each child touch the words as he reads his own sentence to the class. On the next day, have students read the predictable chart again. Have each student read her own sentence. Kindergarten students can do this because they know that each sentence starts with "I like . . ." and finishes with what each student said. The predictability of the sentences helps all students accomplish this task. When you finish, ask students to look at the sentences and point to things they notice. **Students will notice a variety of things, depending upon what they know about letters, sounds, words, and reading.** Their observations may include the following:

All of the sentences begin with **I like.**

French and **fries** begin with the same two letters—**fr.**

Ryan and **Refugio** both start with **R.**

I is at the beginning of each sentence!

I is always a capital letter!

A lot of words have **ing** at the ends.

TV is spelled with two letters: **T** and **V.**

All sentences have this (a period) at the end.

Accept and praise whatever students notice: "Good noticing! TV is made up of two letters. Does anyone know what kind of letters those are?" Point to the chart and ask more questions: "Does anyone know what this mark is called? Why is it placed there?" Offer explanations: "It is called an exclamation point. It is placed there to show that Ryan is excited about school." Students also like to act out their sentences. By reading the names on the chart, students know whose turn is next.

Sentence Builders

- Write a sentence from the chart on a sentence strip with a thick black marker.
- Have a student find the sentence on the chart and match the sentence strip to it.
- Let students watch as you cut the sentence into words.
- Mix up the words for this sentence. Have students use the words to recreate the sentence as it is written on the predictable chart.
- Let students become sentence builders. Choose one student for each word in the sentence and give each student a word card. If you use Emily's sentence, let Emily be her

name at the end of the sentence. Let students stand in front of the class in the same order as the words in the sentence. Read the sentence aloud **after** each student gets in the place where he thinks that he belongs.

- Some students will check the chart and get in the right place; other students will not only find their places quickly, but will also help any student who does not automatically get in the right place!

- Do this with 3–5 sentences on the predictable chart. Use all students' sentences over the next few weeks.

Repeat this procedure for each sentence, giving the words to different students. Ask students to become sentence builders and to get in the right order so that they look like the sentence on the chart. When students get in their places, read the sentence so that students can see if they have completed the task correctly. Let every student be a word during this activity.

Students Building Their Own Sentences and Making a Class Book

The final activity for a predictable chart is creating a class book. Have students reread the predictable chart. Then, give each student an envelope with the words in his sentence inside. Have students sequence the words to make the sentence on the bottom of a piece of drawing paper. Check each sentence to see if it is correct. Then, let each student tape or paste her sentence on the paper. Next, students can illustrate their sentences using markers or crayons. Put these pages in a class book that you and your students can read together. Kindergartners enjoy seeing their work and their classmates' work turned into a book.

Other Ideas for Predictable Charts

In Fall, I see . . . (pumpkins, apples, ghosts, scarecrows, etc.).
For Halloween, I will be a . . . (princess, skeleton, tiger, knight, mermaid, firefighter, etc.).

Writing by Students

Model drawing a picture and writing a sentence. See which students can do this. Don't be upset if they cannot do this; this is only an assessment to see who can. Students will soon be able to do this if you keep up your reading, writing, and phonics instruction.

Getting to Know You

Learning about Letters and Sounds

Getting to Know You usually continues past the first month of school. Teachers continue picking names, interviewing students, cheering each student's name, writing each student's name, and having the class draw pictures of each special student. When you are past the halfway point in adding the names to the wall or bulletin board, let students notice the similarities and differences in the names. Instead of pointing out that Robert's name starts with the same letter and sound as **Ryan**, say "What do you notice about the letters and sounds in Robert's name and the other names?"

There is a system and a pattern in the way letters represent sounds. Instruction should point out these patterns. Students who see a new word and ask themselves how that new word is like other words they know can discover many patterns on their own. Getting to Know You is not just about students getting to know other students, but it is also about them learning about letter-sound relationships in ways that make sense.

Consolidating Letter-Sound Information

What about the letter sounds that have not been represented or covered using the beginning letters of students' names? Are you worried about these letter sounds? Don't be! As you cheered and wrote names, you talked about more than just beginning letters. Now, take a few days to talk about each letter and which students have that letter in their names. Ask, "Whose name has the letter **a** in it?" Let each student who has the letter **a** in her name stand up and say her name. All students listen for **a** and look at the name on the wall or bulletin board. Then, the student who said her name points to the **a** in her name on the wall. Students see that **a** makes a lot of different sounds in names. Move on and ask, "Whose name has **b** in it?" Let each student with **b** in his name stand and tell his name and where **b** is in the name as he points to it on the wall. Students can hear that these names all have the same sound for **b**. "Whose name has **c** in it?" Students notice that **c** has more than one sound. "Whose name has **d** in it?" **D** usually has just one sound, and so on. Continue going through the letters for 3–4 days. This activity reviews letter sounds; makes students aware that some letters have just one sound, some have two or three sounds, and some (vowels) have many sounds; and helps all students consolidate the letter-sound information.

Developing Phonemic Awareness

Rhymes, Chants, and Songs

Have you listened to kindergartners on the playground when they tease each other? Often, you hear chants such as "Silly Billy" and "Saggy, baggy Maggie." Students are becoming aware of words and sounds and can manipulate these to express themselves. **Students and rhymes just go together. Students love to chant, sing, and make up rhymes!**

Most kindergarten teachers have an amazing store of rhymes and fingerplays to go with their units throughout the seasons, such as "One, Two Buckle My Shoe" when learning to count and "Five Little Pumpkins" for October. Doing rhymes with students, however, is not just for fun! **Rhyming activities develop one of the most critical concepts for success in beginning reading—phonemic awareness.** Students like to chant rhymes and do fingerplays that go with the words. Rhyming allows students to listen to the words and learn more about words and how they work.

Remember Michelle, whose favorite book was *In a People House* when she was a little girl? She developed phonemic awareness by the time she was three. At that time, she had imaginary friends whom she named Eedie, Beedie, and Deedie. Michelle had learned how to manipulate letters and sounds to make new names—she was ready for letter-sound instruction (phonics) long before she went to school.

Most students who come to school with well-developed phonemic awareness abilities have had a lot of Dr. Seuss books read to them. Wanting to simulate what happens in literate homes before students come to school, kindergarten teachers develop phonemic awareness by using books such as the following:

The Ear Book by Al Perkins (Random House, 1968)

The Foot Book by Dr. Seuss (Random House, 1968)

Hop on Pop by Dr. Seuss (Random House, 1963)

One Fish Two Fish Red Fish Blue Fish by Dr. Seuss (Random House, 1960)

Phonemic Awareness Songs and Rhymes: Fall by Kimberly Jordano and Trisha Callella (Creative Teaching Press, 1998)

There's a Wocket in My Pocket by Dr. Seuss (Random House, 1974)

Another rhyming big book that kindergartners love is *Golden Bear* by Ruth Young (Puffin, 1994). It is the story of an adorable boy and his teddy bear. The boy sees his bear everywhere: on a stair and in a chair; playing a violin under his chin; on a rug with a bug; and on the ice making circles twice. Let students tell you the rhyming pairs that they hear in this book as you read it to them.

After reading and rereading the book, help students come up with some other rhyming places where Golden Bear might be found. Can the bear be found in the park after dark, in school being cool, or in the car with a jar? This activity of finding rhyming words can be done with any rhyming book you read to the class.

Rhymes are not just for reading—rhymes are for having fun! As students participate in shared reading and writing, they become aware of words as separate entities. **Using fingerplays with rhyming words, reading rhyming books, and talking about rhyming words give all students a chance to increase their phonemic awareness.**

> The ability to make up rhymes and play with words is one of the most reliable indicators that students are getting control of language.

Reading Rhyming Books and Finding Rhymes

Reading rhyming books helps students develop a sense of rhyme and phonemic awareness. Here are three books you can read to the class early in the year. Remember that you can also read to your class any rhyming books from your classroom library.

10 Fat Turkeys by Tony Johnson (Cartwheel, 2004)
This is a silly book that counts backward from 10 turkeys falling off of a fence one by one until there are none. You can talk about rhyming words as you read this book and help students find the rhyming words after reading the book.

Oink! Moo! How Do You Do? A Book of Animal Sounds by Grace Maccarone (Scholastic, 1994)
First, read the book and enjoy it. Then, find the rhyming words (**Moo/do, haw/saw, tweet/eat, meow/now, neigh/way, cock-a-doodle-doo/too, cluck/luck, ruff/enough, shoo/you, quack/back, buzz/was, cheep/sleep**). Note: This book can be found only in the school market.

I Love Trains! by Philemon Sturges (HarperCollins, 2001)
This book about trains is written in rhyme. Read the book and enjoy it. Then, reread the book and help students find the rhyming words (**roar/door, strong/along, rain/grain, hogs/logs, scrap/wrap, end/bend**; **glad/Dad**).

October

Centers

It's October, so fall, colors, and Halloween are topics of learning centers this month. (Using Halloween as a topic depends upon where you live and the students you teach!)

Reading Center

Fill the Reading Center with books on October topics. Include some books that have been read to the class and some that have not. The Reading Center gives students a chance to hold the books and see the words and pictures about the themes they are discussing. **Some students will look at the pictures and learn, and other students will pretend read and learn.** Books read by the teacher and placed in the Reading Center will help these students. Students who can already read become more fluent at reading. A lot of easy readers and simple text will help.

Writing Center

Fill the walls of the Writing Center with charts for color and fall words. In the Writing Center, one activity students can make is an October Picture Dictionary using the words from the charts or bulletin board (see also Carson-Dellosa's *Building Blocks "Plus" for Kindergarten Bulletin Board*). **Some students will copy the words from the charts and draw pictures to match the words. Other students will use pencils, markers, and crayons to scribble, draw, "drite," and write the words depending on where they are in their writing development.** When students finish, staple together each student's pages so that every student will have a little book he can take home.

Since entering kindergarten, most students have learned more about writing and about how to write. They enjoy the Writing Center because it is a place where they can practice what they have learned and where their efforts will be rewarded with a smile and kind words.

Books and writing materials should be in every center. Encourage students to build pictures that they see in books with the blocks in the Blocks Center and draw pictures of their finished products. Have them make grocery lists and write messages in the Home Center. Let students label what they create in the Art Center. Show them that reading and writing happens everywhere!

November

November is the month during which teachers realize that although students have finally settled into the daily routine, holidays will be here soon! From this point forward, it seems as if there is never enough time for teachers to do everything that they want to do and read every book that they want to read. In this chapter, we focus on learning more about letters, sounds, and words through shared reading and writing. In the United States, discussing Thanksgiving and all of the things for which we are thankful can take up a big part of November. Some classes study families and how families have changed over time, and some classes study food, food groups, and nutrition in November.

The Opening

The Opening has become routine, and all students have had time to listen to and become familiar with these procedures. Students know what will be talked about each morning and are comfortable with the usual questions they have encountered since school began: questions about the calendar, days of the week, date, month, seasons, and types of weather. Students are willing to take turns talking and answering questions during The Opening. When asked, "What do you notice?" about a particular sentence or group of words, students' answers show their growth in letter, letter-sound, and word knowledge. You have been working hard to teach these concepts, and your efforts are paying off. For this, you are thankful!

Reading Aloud to Students

November is a good month to read stories and new informational books about a variety of subjects.

When learning about families, there are many books you can read to students. *Alexander and the Terrible, Horrible, No Good, Very Bad Day* by Judith Viorst (Aladdin, 1972) is a story about a traditional family. All students (and adults!) relate to this story because we have all had days like Alexander's! If you want to read about a family from long ago, read *Ox-Cart Man* by Donald Hall (Puffin, 1979). Another book is *Alexander, Who's Not (Do You Hear Me? I Mean It!) Going to Move* by Judith Viorst (Aladdin, 1995) about a family who is moving and a little boy who does not want to move. For classes with students who have recently moved or have someone who will be moving soon, this is a good book to read.

For students whose extended families living in the same house, do not forget the stories that Tomie dePaola writes about his grandmothers, *Nana Upstairs Nana Downstairs* (Putnam Juvenile, 1973) and *Watch Out for the Chicken Feet in Your Soup* (Aladdin, 1974). Also, *Song and Dance Man* by Karen Ackerman (Knopf Books for Young Readers, 1988) is a wonderful story of a grandfather with a colorful past.

November ···

Many students can relate to the book *The Relatives Came* by Cynthia Rylant (Aladdin, 1985). While reading books about families, students may want to talk about their mothers, fathers, sisters, brothers, grandparents, and anyone with whom they live or whom they love. To help students learn about changing families, read *Dinosaurs Divorce: A Guide for Changing Families* by Laurene Krasny Brown and Marc Brown (Little, Brown Young Readers, 1986).

Multicultural stories include *More More More Said the Baby* by Vera B. Williams (HarperTrophy, 1990), *Everette Anderson's Nine Months Long* by Lucille Clifton (Henry Holt and Company, 1988), *A Chair for My Mother* by Vera Williams (HarperTrophy, 1984), and *Mama, Do You Love Me?* by Barbara M. Joosse (Chronicle, 1991). *Mama, Do You Love Me?* is about an Inuit child who discovers that her mother's love for her is unconditional. *Just Like Daddy* by Frank Asch (Aladdin, 1981) is a story about a little bear who tries to be like his dad from the start of a day until he catches a fish—just like Mommy!

Young children love Mercer Mayer's Little Critter books because they can relate to the issues of growing up. Some books in this series are *Just Me and My Dad, Just Me and My Mom, Just Me and My Puppy, Just Me in the Tub, The New Baby, When I Get Bigger, Just Go to Bed, Just a Mess, Just Grandpa and Me, Just Grandma and Me, I Just Forgot, I Was So Mad, I'm Sorry,* and *Just a New Neighbor.* (For publisher information on these books, see pages 162–172.)

When studying food and how some food grows, there are many books to read. *Growing Vegetable Soup* by Lois Ehlert (Harcourt, 1987) is one. After reading this book, plan to grow some vegetable soup of your own with the class. Parents can be invited to share this simple feast at school. While planning and writing the menu, you have another opportunity to call attention to letters, sounds, and words: "What will we put in our soup? Carrots, green beans, tomatoes, onions, corn, peas, and potatoes are good choices. How can we sort the vegetables that we are putting in our soup? Which vegetable names begin alike? Which vegetables are the same color?" Kindergarten students enjoy learning through reading—just like adults!

Continue to read alphabet books, rhyming books, and familiar tales that students will be expected to know: *The Little Red Hen, Little Red Riding Hood, The Three Bears, The Three Little Pigs, Three Billy Goats Gruff,* and *The Gingerbread Boy.*

More Books to Read in November

An Alphabet Salad: Fruits and Vegetables from A to Z by Sarah L. Schuette (Capstone Press, 2003)

Growing Colors by Bruce McMillan (HarperTrophy, 1994)

Molly's Pilgrim by Barbara Cohen (HarperCollins, 1995)

One Tough Turkey by Steven Kroll (Holiday House, 1982)

The Popcorn Book by Tomie dePaola (Holiday House, 1984)

Thanksgiving Day by Gail Gibbons (Holiday House, 1985)

Today Is Thanksgiving by P. K. Hallinan (Ideals Publications, 1993)

What Is Thanksgiving? by Harriet Ziefert (HarperCollins, 1992)

Reading with Students
Shared Reading with Predictable Big Books

There are some great nonfiction big books. Try to include both fiction and nonfiction in your big book selection each month. If the big books are predictable, they are even better. Some books, such as *Things I Like* by Anthony Browne (Dragonfly Books, 1989), are predictable because of the pictures. Other books, such as *Brown Bear, Brown Bear, What Do You See?* by Bill Martin Jr. (Henry Holt and Company, 1967) have predictable patterns. Still other books have both predictable pictures and text, such as *The Little Red Hen*. Byron Barton's (HarperTrophy, 1996) beautifully illustrated retelling of the well-known tale was selected for this activity. You might also choose a version by Paul Galdone (Clarion, 2006) or Margot Zemarch (Farrar, Straus and Giroux, 1993). In Barton's version, the little red hen's friends would rather play than work. When the hen asks who will help her plant seeds, cut the stalks, thresh the wheat, grind the grain, and make flour into bread, her friends repeatedly reply, "Not I." But, they have a different answer when she asks who will help her eat the bread she makes!

The Little Red Hen is a wonderful book for shared reading in kindergarten. **The story is predictable, it does not have too much print, and the sentence patterns are repetitious. The pictures support the familiar sentence patterns.** The story also appeals to students because they have all either said "Not I" or wanted to at some time. You can read this book during November to tie into a family, food, or Thanksgiving theme.

Before Reading

Take a picture walk through the book. Talk about the animals in the story and what they are doing—or not doing! Let the pictures help you figure out the character words **hen**, **cat**, and **pig**.

During Reading

The first time you read the book to your class, let students listen to the story and enjoy it. You may want to reread this story and talk about what the little red hen does when she finds some seeds—and why she does this. This will help students understand the steps involved in turning wheat into flour, and it will also set the mood for the story. The third time you read the story, students will want to join in. They know that the answer each time will be "Not I."

Read each page in the big book again, stopping to talk about what students notice about the print. Some responses you hear may include the following:

"The words **Not I** are there a lot."

"**Cat** and **cut** begin with **c**."

"**Cat**, **pig**, and **hen** each have just three letters!"

"**Day** and **duck** start with **d**."

"**Me** and **make** both start with the **m** sound, like **Miranda**."

Ask students about the quotation marks if they do not mention them. Not all students are ready to learn about quotation marks, but some are and pointing them out makes this activity more multilevel.

Remember to have students listen or read for a purpose each time.

- "As I read this story, listen to find out what the little red hen does when she finds some seeds."

- "As we read the story this time, listen to what the hen does to make bread. We will talk about it and make a list after we read."

- "As we read today, think about which animal you would like to be when we act out the story."

After Reading

After reading, work on comprehension. Discuss the story by asking students, "What happens in the story? Why?" Sequence the events. "What happens to the little red hen first? Next? Then? Finally?" Don't ask just literal questions. Even kindergartners can answer big questions, such as "Who works the hardest in this story?" That will make them think beyond the literal.

Your class will want to act out this story! Let several students become the characters and act out the story as you reread it. Make yarned character cards, worn like necklaces, or animal puppets. You can make simple animal puppets by gluing small drawings of the animals on craft sticks. Reread the story several times, giving different students chances to be the characters. Students love acting out this story and saying, "Not I." By rereading the story, students become familiar with the story and can then read or pretend read the book on their own.

Informational Text

One choice for a nonfiction shared-reading book in November might be *Pilgrims of Plymouth* by Susan Goodman (National Geographic Children's Books, 1999). Most kindergarten students in the United States know that some people eat turkey on Thanksgiving Day, and may know that they should be thankful for things on Thanksgiving Day. What else do they know about this holiday? Reading this big book will help students travel back in time to meet the Pilgrims and learn what life was like for the people who came to America in the 17th century.

When you look at the text, remember that the purpose of shared reading for students is not to learn how to read all of the words in the book but to be able to join in and share the reading of some of the text. The part that students read is usually the predictable, repetitive text, and they are asked to do this after they have heard the text at least once. When reading this text, it may be a good time to tell students that even adult readers don't always read a whole book in one day.

Day 1: Cover and Pages 1–9

Before Reading
Just like with fiction, the cover of a nonfiction text gives us the title, the author, and a picture to talk about. Do the cover talk and picture walk with nonfiction books also. With this book, you might ask, "What did you know about the Pilgrims before we read this book?" and "Do you think what happens in this book is real or make-believe? Did the author make it up?" You might also explain that although the pictures were taken recently, everything looks like it took place a long time ago when the Pilgrims lived. You do not need to go into great detail with each picture or page, because you will revisit these pages several times. Each time you read the book, talk more about what is happening in the pictures.

During Reading
Read the book to the class or read the first nine pages to learn what Pilgrim men, women, and children did. When students read nonfiction, they are reading to learn something. In this book, they are learning about the Pilgrims and what they did. This is enough for kindergarten students to learn in one day. Read the first nine pages again and let students do shared reading. Remind them to let the pictures help them read about what the men, women, and children did on these pages.

After Reading
See if students can tell you what has happened in the text so far in their own words. Ask literal questions, such as, "Where and when did this take place? What did Pilgrim men do? What did Pilgrim women do? What did Pilgrim children do?" Get students to think by asking, "Did you learn something today that you did not know before we read this book?" Kindergarten is not too early to introduce a KWL chart. In kindergarten, is not a written activity; it is an oral one.

Before Reading
K: "What do you know about the Pilgrims?"
W: "What do you want to learn or wonder about the Pilgrims?"

After Reading
L: "What did you learn about the Pilgrims?" Follow this reading and discussion by giving each child a piece of paper on which they will draw something that Pilgrim men did, something that Pilgrim women did, and something that Pilgrim children did (see reproducible on page 49).

···

Day 2: Pages 10–16

Before Reading

Ask, "What did we learn about the Pilgrims yesterday?" Be sure that the discussion includes what students learned about Pilgrim men, women, and children. "Let's see what we will read about today." Talk about what is in the pictures in the remainder of the book and what students think they might learn about the Pilgrims today.

During Reading

Read pages 10–16 to the class. Then, read it again and have students join in and share the reading of what the Indians (or Native Americans, as they are often called today) did (pages 10–11) and how the Pilgrims were different from and like people today (pages 14–15).

After Reading

Ask students what they learned today in their reading. Have students discuss how the Indians helped the Pilgrims and ask students to draw pictures showing this.

Day 3: Reread the Book

Before Reading

Review the book by discussing what students learned about the Pilgrims.

During Reading

Do a shared reading of the entire book. "Let's read this book again together to see if we remembered everything."

After Reading

Discuss the book. "Did we forget to tell something we learned before we read? How were the Pilgrims like us? How were they different?" On a piece of paper, have students draw how the Pilgrims were different from us and how the Pilgrims were like us (see reproducible on page 50).

Name_____ Date_____

1. Draw something that Pilgrim men did.

2. Draw something that Pilgrim women did.

3. Draw something that Pilgrim children did.

Name_____ Date_____

1. Draw how the Pilgrims were different from us.

2. Draw how the Pilgrims were like us.

Writing for Students

Morning Message

Morning Messages written after students have been in school for a while might look like the following:

> Dear Class,
>
> Thursday is a holiday.
>
> It is Thanksgiving.
>
> We do not have school!
>
> Love,
>
> Mrs. Hall

> Dear Class,
>
> Last Thursday was Thanksgiving.
>
> My daughters came to visit.
>
> What did you do for Thanksgiving?
>
> Love,
>
> Mrs. Hall

During this time of year, you may write the Morning Message and not spell every word. You may ask, "Who can tell me what letter I write first when writing **Dear**?" Or, write **Dear Class**," and ask, "Who can read what I just wrote?" Some days, write the opening and closing lines without saying them aloud and ask if anyone can read them. After 40–50 days, most students know what you write to begin and end the Morning Message. The smiles on their faces show how proud they are of this accomplishment. Choose a student to read the opening and closing. Then, praise his reading. Also, try to use more than one kind of sentence so that students see periods, question marks, and exclamation points being used.

After writing and reading the Morning Message, ask students several of the following questions:

- Who can count the sentences? Words?
- Which sentence is the longest? Shortest?
- What do you notice about the Morning Message?
- Who can find a word she knows in the Morning Message?
- Who can find a word in the Morning Message that rhymes with ___?
- Who can tell me how that word starts (what letter or letters)?
- What letter do I need to write first? Next?
- What kind of letter does **Dear** begin with?
- What kind of letter goes at the beginning of each sentence?
- What kind of sentence is this?
- What do I put at the end of this sentence?

Journal Entry at the End of the Day

One way to begin journal writing is to end each day by talking about what your class did that day and writing about it while students watch. Many teachers end each day with a class meeting to discuss what happened that day. This helps students answer when they are asked, "What did you do in school today?" You can spend a few minutes talking about the day and write down some things. Talking about, writing, and reading this journal entry makes the question easier for many students to answer. It also gives you another opportunity to write for students before asking them to do it.

First, write the date. Next, discuss the events of the day. You may need to help students organize the events in the correct order and decide what to write about (you cannot write every detail). Then, write these sentences on a piece of chart paper.

> November 2, 2009
>
> Today, we began school with big group. Next, we heard a story. Then, we made a page for our class book about our families. We went to P.E. and had math. We ended our day with centers.

As you write, talk about what you are doing and why.

"My first sentence is about the first thing we did today."

"I start each sentence with a capital letter because sentences always begin that way."

Writing a journal entry at the end of each day helps students focus on some important things they did that day. To get students ready to spell words, model spelling daily during your journal entry. When you begin words like **made** or **math**, say, "This word begins like **Madison**. We know that words that begin like **Madison** begin with **m**." Stretch out the words as you say and spell them so that students can hear the sounds as they watch you write the letters.

> When you write for students, you provide a model for them. Later, when they are asked to write their own journal entries, they will know what is expected of them and how to do it.

Writing with Students

Predictable Charts

After reading *The Little Red Hen*, make a predictable chart about how students like to help (I can help . . .). Following a story about the first Thanksgiving or Thanksgiving today, write another predictable chart by talking about the things for which students are thankful. Start with a piece of chart paper and write **I Am Thankful For . . .** at the top.

As each student tells something for which she is thankful, write it on the chart, followed by the student's name in parentheses. On the last line, write something for which you are thankful.

I Am Thankful For . . .

I am thankful for my mommy. (Adam)   I am thankful for my family. (Emily)

I am thankful for my sister. (Madison)   I am thankful for my home. (Mitchell)

I am thankful for french fries. (Jasmine)   I am thankful for my grandma. (Nikki)

I am thankful for my teddy bear. (Erica)   I am thankful for everything! (Paul)

I am thankful for Tommy, my cat. (Suzanne)   I am thankful for my teacher. (Tiara)

I am thankful for my dog. (Ryan)   I am thankful for good food. (Julie)

I am thankful for school. (Refugio)   I am thankful for my Nana and Grampy. (Jimmy)

I am thankful for food. (William)   I am thankful for my new house. (Rashawn)

I am thankful for turkey. (Mike)   I am thankful for my trailer. (Christopher)

I am thankful for my friends. (Olivia)   I am thankful for my class! (Miss Williams)

I am thankful for my daddy. (Jacob)

If you have time when you have finished the shared writing of this predictable chart, read the chart from beginning to end with students.

Touch Reading

The next day, students are ready to read their sentences, alone or with help, and to talk about the things that they notice. One by one, students read the sentences they dictated and touch each word on the chart as they read it. When asked what they notice, several students point out that **mommy,** and **my** start with **m**. Some students know that **teddy, teacher,** and **Tommy** begin with the same letter and sound. Another student may notice that **Thanksgiving** begins with the same letter but does not have the same beginning sound as **teddy, teacher,** and **Tommy**. Many students can read the words **I Am Thankful For . . .** at the beginning of the chart and each sentence without any help. Most students know that the ending mark after each sentence is a period. Some students even know why you put it there.

Sentence Builders

The following day, choose two or three sentences, write them on sentence strips, cut apart the words for each sentence, and put them in separate resealable plastic bags. Kindergartners love to get in front of the class and build the sentences from the chart with the words that you give them. After students build a sentence, read it aloud to check that students are in the correct order. Let students build several sentences from the predictable chart. Then, call attention to some letters, sounds, or words that you want to discuss.

What Do You Notice?

To focus attention on beginning letters and sounds, have the class go on an **m** hunt and find **m** words on the chart. Or, ask students to find all of the **d** words on the chart that begin like **David**. It is a more multilevel approach to ask, "What do you notice?" The question stretches the minds of students who know letter-sound relationships, as well as those of students who are not yet aware of them.

Making a Class Book

On the fourth day, students will place and paste their sentences on pieces of paper. Once this is complete, students will illustrate their sentences. Every student will have a page in the class book. Place the book in the Reading Center where all students can read and enjoy it. Some other books to use for making predictable charts in November are the following:

I Am Special by Kimberly Jordano (Creative Teaching Press, 1996)

Look What I Can Do by Jose Aruego (Aladdin, 1971)

We Can Share at School by Rozanne Lanczak Williams (Creative Teaching Press, 1996)

Getting to Know You

Connecting Students' Names to Letters and Sounds

By the end of November, every student will have had a chance to be in the spotlight, to take home pictures that her classmates drew of her, and to have her name put on the special student bulletin board. A class-made book, *Our Class*, is in the Reading Center, and some students can read all of the names.

Second Round: Interactive Charts

Most teachers say that one round of Getting to Know You is not enough, because students love this activity. The second time, you may want to use the chart in the *Building Blocks "Plus" for Kindergarten Bulletin Board* (Carson-Dellosa, 1998) or make your own interactive charts. For more information on interactive charts, see *Interactive Charts* by Dorothy Hall and Karen Loman (Carson-Dellosa, 2002).

You will need four sentences:

My name is _____.

I am _____ years old.

My favorite color is _____.

I like to eat _____.

Choose one student each day. He cheers his name from memory. Then, have him complete each sentence. Once all students have done this second round, place the chart above in the Reading Center with the typical responses from which to choose written on index cards. (You should include each student's name for the first line; numerals four, five, and six for the second line; color words written in the matching colors for the third line; and favorite foods and pictures of the foods for the last line.)

Learning Words: Rote Memory and Associative Memory

There are two kinds of learning based on the brain's two types of memory stores. Things we do repeatedly until we learn them are put in our **rote-memory stores. This rote-memory store has a limited capacity, and if we do not practice something in rote memory for a while, then the rote memory gives that information's space to something more current.** (What was her phone number? Before she went to Florida, I called her every day and knew it, but now I will have to look it up again!) **The other memory store, the associative store, has unlimited capacity. We can find things in the associative memory store that we have not thought about for years if the memory is triggered by the right image, smell, song, etc. The trick to putting information in the associative store rather than in the rote store is to make an association with the information.**

Students who are trying to remember that a particular shape turned a particular way is called **d** and that it has the same beginning sound as **doughnut** and **dog** cannot make associations between the name and sound of **d** with **doughnut** and **dog** unless they can read the words **doughnut** and **dog**. These students may try to remember that it is called **d** and has the sound of **doughnut** and **dog**. When they do this, they put all of this information into their rote-memory stores, and if they do not use it for a while, the space in their rote memory will be used by something else. Then, students will have to learn the letter and sound information again!

The only way to help students put letter-name and sound knowledge in their associative stores rather than their rote stores is to make sure that they can read some words that contain the letters. If all students' names are on the special student bulletin board, use these names as associative links to letter names and sounds.

November $\cdots\cdots\cdots\cdots\cdots\cdots\cdots\cdots\cdots\cdots\cdots\cdots\cdots\cdots\cdots\cdots\cdots\cdots\cdots\cdots\cdots$

Imagine that the names of students displayed on the wall or bulletin board are the following:

Jasmine	Ryan	Michelle	Mike	Adam
Erica	Suzanne	Refugio	William	Olivia
Jacob	Emily	Mitchell	Nikki	Paul
Tiara	Julie	Jimmy	Rashawn	Victor

Write students' names on cards or sentence strips and pass them out to the correct students. **Begin with a letter that many students have in their names and that usually has its expected sound.** With this class, you might begin with **r**. Have all students whose names have **r** in them come to the front of the classroom holding their name cards or sentence strips. First, count the **r**'s. There are six **r**'s. Next, have students whose names contain **r** divide themselves into those whose names begin with **r** (Ryan, Rashawn, and Refugio), end with **r** (Victor), and have **r** somewhere else (Erica, Tiara). Finally, say each name slowly and help students decide if they can hear the usual sound of that letter. For **r**, you can hear the usual sound in all of these names.

Now, choose another letter and let students whose names have that letter come to the front of the classroom and display their name cards. Count the number of times the letter occurs and have students divide themselves into groups according to whether the letter is the first letter in their names, the last letter, or in between. Finally, stretch out the names and help students decide if they can hear the usual letter sound. The letter **m** would be a good second choice for this list of names. **Mitchell**, **Michelle**, and **Mike** begin with **m**, **Adam** and **William** end with **m**, and **Jasmine**, **Emily**, and **Jimmy** have **m**'s that are not the first or last letters. Again, you can hear the usual sound of **m** in all of these names.

Continue picking letters and having students come to the front of the classroom with their name cards. Do not try to do all of the letters in one day, just those represented in several names.

Developing Phonemic Awareness

Rhyming Books

Most young students who have been read to can hear rhymes, and often ask the reader to reread pages or to repeat rhymes. Many of us remember nursery rhymes because we have heard them so many times! We also noticed the rhyming words at the ends of lines. In Dr. Seuss's Beginner Books, students cannot help but hear the rhymes. When you read these books to students, they often begin to guess the next rhyming word because they are paying such close attention to both the pictures and the print.

An example of one of these books is Dr. Seuss's *Green Eggs and Ham* (Random House, 1960). It is about a character named Sam-I-am and eating green eggs and ham. The first reading is always for the pleasure of hearing the story. From the first page, students listen to the words and begin to hear the rhymes. After several pages, even students without much print experience can hear the rhyming words: "I do not like them in a house. I do not like them with a mouse. I do not like them here or there. I do not like them anywhere. I do not like green eggs and ham. I do not like them, Sam-I-am." After reading the story and talking about it, reread it to find the rhyming words. The rhymes repeat several times, making pairs of rhyming words easy to spot. Read some other rhyming books this month and find the rhyming words with students.

Favorite Rhyming Books

Annie Bananie by Leah Komaiko (HarperTrophy, 1987)

Ape in a Cape: An Alphabet of Odd Animals by Fritz Eichenberg (Voyager, 1952)

A Bug in a Jug and Other Funny Rhymes by Gloria Patrick (Scholastic, 1970)

Each Peach Pear Plum by Janet Ahlberg and Allan Ahlberg (Puffin, 1978)

Everette Anderson's Nine Months Long by Lucille Clifton (Henry Holt and Company, 1988)

Golden Bear by Ruth Young (Puffin, 1994)

Hop on Pop by Dr. Seuss (Random House, 1963)

Jake Baked the Cake by B. G. Hennessy (Puffin, 1992)

One Fish Two Fish Red Fish Blue Fish by Dr. Seuss (Random House, 1960)

Pretend You're a Cat by Jean Marzollo (Dial, 1990)

Centers

Reading Center

The Reading Center contains many books about Thanksgiving, families, and food. It also contains class-made books from predictable charts. Students read these books by themselves and to friends when they are in the Reading Center. Some students try to read newspapers and magazines just as they have seen grown-ups do. Often, a child pretends that he is the teacher and shares a book that he can read just like the teacher does in class—he reads the text and shows the pictures.

Writing Center

The Writing Center has a November Picture Dictionary chart or bulletin board on the wall (see *Building Blocks "Plus" for Kindergarten Bulletin Board* from Carson-Dellosa). There is also a chart with pictures and names of people, places, and events from the first Thanksgiving.

Students find new Thanksgiving-themed stamps and an ink pad in the Writing Center. Many students will draw and write using the stamps. Others will use the stamps to create pictures, then color and decorate the pictures. Some students write the things for which they are thankful, just like you did as a class. With stamps, pictures, and print, students get their messages on paper. When you listen to, look at, and praise these early attempts at writing, students begin to see themselves as writers.

Assessing Progress

Assessment is an ongoing process for experienced kindergarten teachers who have become good student watchers.

- As students respond to various activities, notice who can do what. If you write what you notice, you will have anecdotal records!

- Samples—particularly writing samples—are also informative. By comparing early and later samples of a student's work, growth can be determined and validated.

In kindergarten, most teachers want to do individual student assessments. What you assess and how you do it should mirror your instruction. Some tasks that will help you assess the concepts on which you have been concentrating are included in this chapter. Some students will be able to complete all of these tasks successfully. Hopefully, every child will be able to do at least some of the tasks. Before you begin your assessment, make sure that you have all of the necessary materials. Then, decide when you will do the assessment and how many students you will assess each day. **Assessment should not take too long; try to finish assessing your entire class in one week. Center time is usually a good time to do individual assessments.**

Here are some things you should assess at this point of kindergarten:

Assessing Words

Students who are progressing should have learned some words used in daily activities, including the names of their classmates and words used in The Opening. Most students will not have learned all of the names or The Opening words, but some students will have learned all of them. To assess word learning, write the first names of students on index cards. Put them in a pocket chart or spread them out on the table. Ask each child to choose three to five name cards and read them to you. **Students who can read three to five names are making progress with word learning.** Some students will want to read more.

Do a similar activity with words used in The Opening. Write some words you use each day during The Opening, including **the days of the week and weather words**. Ask each child to read the names of three to five days of the week and three weather words (**sunny**, **cloudy**, **rainy**).

Assessing Letter Names

You have been talking about letters and letter names during The Opening, when working with students' names, when writing, when reading big books, and when asking, "What do you notice?" **It is now time to see if students recognize some letter names.** It is not necessary for students to know all 52 uppercase and lowercase letters at this time, but they should have learned some of them. Make copies of page 64 or write six unconfusing capital letters (**A**, **D**, **B**, **M**, **S**, and **R**) and six lowercase letters (**o**, **i**, **e**, **c**, **t**, and **n**) separately on index cards. **Ask each student to pick up and name as many letters as she can.** If this task seems easy for many students, add more letters.

November

Assessing Phonemic Awareness

You have been clapping the syllables in students' names and working with the concept of rhyme. Find out if students are progressing in these two areas of phonemic awareness.

Choose several students' names, each with a different number of syllables. Ask each child to say each name and clap the beats. For example, if you said **Jasmine**, the student would repeat the name and clap twice. The child would also clap twice for **Ryan**. For **Paul**, the child would clap once.

To assess rhyme, make copies of page 63 or collect six pictures of common objects that have rhyming names.

> bike   bed   cat   cake   van   bus

Name the six pictures with the child. Then, have the child name them. Next, tell the child that you will say a name and he should repeat the name and find a picture that rhymes with it. Do one together as an example:

"The first name is **Ted**. Say **Ted** and the names of the pictures. Which picture name rhymes with **Ted**?"

Help the child realize that **Ted** and **bed** rhyme. Have the child say **"Ted–bed"** several times and remove the bed picture. Now, there are five pictures left.

Name each picture and have the child repeat each name and find the picture that rhymes with each of the following names:

> Mike   Pat   Jake   Dan   Gus

To assess beginning sounds, have each student listen to two words and ask her if the words begin alike. Say the following pairs:

Billy, birthday	Jasmine, jump	bike, ball	Chad, cherries	cat, cup
Billy, cake	Jasmine, walk	bike, magic	Chad, bananas	cat, dog

Assessing Print Concepts

Reading requires particular ways of moving the eyes and an understanding of jargon, such as **word**, **letter**, etc. Often, students who do not come from literacy-rich homes are confused by the jargon. Although all students speak in words, they do not know that words exist as separate entities until they start reading and writing at school. **To many students, *letters* are what you get in the mailbox; *sounds* are horns, bells, and slamming doors; and *a sentence* is what a person serves if she commits a crime!** These students may be unable to follow your instructions because you are using words that, for them, either have no meaning or have different meanings. All year, you have helped students develop the concepts and jargon of print that they need to progress in reading. Now, it is time to assess how their print concepts are developing.

For this assessment, use a predictable book that was used for shared reading or use a class big book that you created from a predictable chart. **First, ask a student to show you the front of the book. Turn to the first page and ask him to point to where he would start to read. Then, have him point to words for you to read them. Notice if he is pointing to just one word at a time and making the correct return sweep.**

Next, ask him to **point to just one word anywhere on the page**. Then, **have him point to the first word on the page, then the last word on the page**. Ask him to **point to just one letter anywhere on the page**. Then, pick a word from the page and **ask him to point to the first letter of the word and the last letter of the word**.

Using Assessment Results

Use the Kindergarten Assessment Checklist assessment record sheet (page 62) or create your own. Analyze the progress of each child. On a class summary sheet, list students who do not seem to be progressing as quickly as they should. Put this sheet in a place where you will see it often and use it as a reminder for whom to focus on during activities for the upcoming month. While reading big books or predictable charts, ask students who still cannot track print to be pointers during the activity. Help these students show just one word, the last word in the sentence, and so on. Likewise, during the Morning Message and other activities with words, move students who need work with word learning and letter-name knowledge closer to you and call on them more often. Provide individual coaching and nudges to these students as you work with the class. Ask students whose syllable-clapping and rhyming responses indicate difficulty in developing phonemic awareness to lead rhyming and clapping activities with you. Also, work individually or in a small group with students who still need additional time and practice by rereading big books or charts and by focusing on these concepts, especially during center time. At the end of next month, reassess students about whose progress you are concerned, concentrating on the concepts with which the students had problems.

November

Kindergarten Assessment Checklist

Name:	NOV.	JAN.	MAR.	MAY/JUNE
Words				
Student recognizes:				
5 names				
most names				
all names				
Student recognizes:				
5 days of the week				
7 days of the week				
Student recognizes:				
3 weather words				
all weather words				
Letter Names				
A B C D E F G H I J K L M N O P Q R S T U V W X Y Z				
a b c d e f g h i j k l m n o p q r s t u v w x y z				
Phonemic Awareness				
Claps the beats for:				
3 names				
most names				
all names				
Matches pictures with rhyming words				
Can hear words that start alike				
Concepts of Print*				
Finds the front of a book				
Starts on the left side of the page				
Goes left to right across the page				
Makes the return sweep to the next line				
Matches words by pointing to each word when reading				
Points to just one word				
Points to the first and last words				
Points to just one letter				
Points to the first and last letters of a word				
Comments				

*Put a plus (+) to indicate if a student can recognize or complete the task. Once a student has two pluses in a row, there is no need to assess the skill again.

Picture Cards for Assessing Phonemic Awareness

Letter Cards for Assessing Letter Names

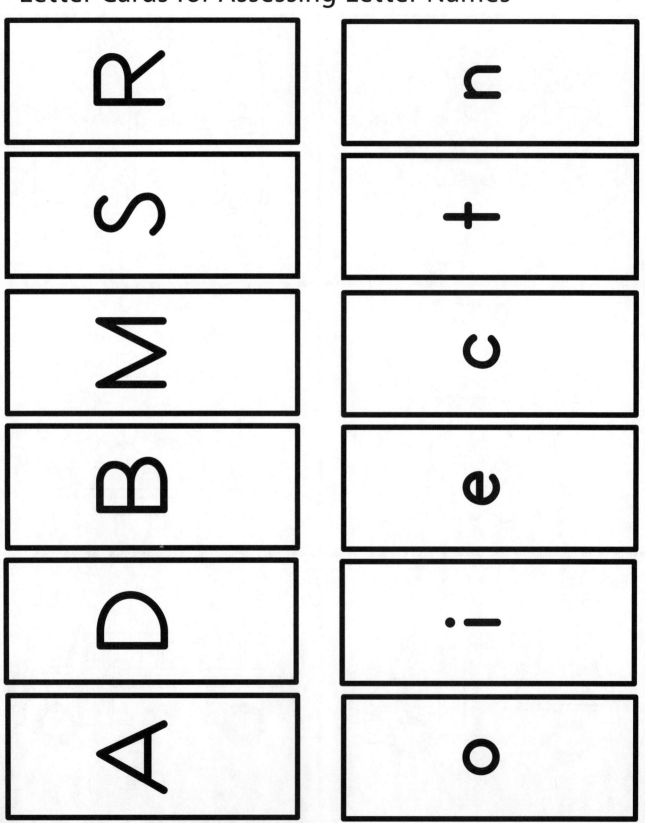

R   n

S   t

M   c

B   e

D   i

A   o

 · · · · · · · **CD-104274 • Month-by-Month Reading, Writing, and Phonics in Kindergarten**

December

December is always a busy month—both at home and at school! The holidays (Christmas, Hanukkah, Kwanzaa, and others) are almost here, and you can use students' interest and enthusiasm for upcoming events to do more reading, writing, and working with words.

The Opening

The Opening is when kindergarten classes discuss this busy month! Students are aware of The Opening routine by now, and their excitement for the season may show. They may notice that **Santa** starts like **Saturday** and **Sunday** and **Merry** starts like **Monday**! Some students may even notice that **Christmas**, **Kwanzaa**, and **Hanukkah** all start with capital letters. Talking about holidays fills The Opening each morning. Teachers and students look at the calendar and count the days until vacation.

Reading Aloud to Students

Reading to students about the holidays capitalizes on their enthusiasm for the season and helps calm them while you read to them in big group. Activities in centers can focus on the stories or the holidays and ideas about which students are learning.

There are many books that can teach students about holidays and the ways people celebrate holidays in different parts of the United States, Canada, and around the world.

Books about Holidays and Celebrations

Bear Stays Up for Christmas by Karma Wilson (Margaret K. McElderry, 2004)

Celebrate Hanukkah: With Light, Latkes, and Dreidels by Deborah Heiligman (National Geographic Children's Books, 2006)

Christmas Time by Gail Gibbons (Holiday House, 1982)

Corduroy's Christmas by Don Freeman and B. G. Hennessy (Scholastic, 1993)

Merry Christmas, Little Critter! by Mercer Mayer (HarperFestival, 2004)

Nine Days to Christmas: A Story of Mexico by Marie Hall Ets and Aurora Labastida (Puffin, 1991)

Seven Spools of Thread by Angela Shelf Medearis (Albert Whitman and Company, 2000)

Too Many Tamales by Gary Soto and Ed Martinez (Putnam Juvenile, 1993)

Reading with Students

Shared Reading with Predictable Big Books

Goodnight Moon by Margaret Wise Brown (HarperTrophy, 2007) is a bedtime favorite. With its repetition, rhyme, and pictures that support the print, this story is a perfect choice for shared reading. In the story, a little rabbit tries to prolong bedtime by saying good night to everything in sight. The story is also a rhythmic review of color words and rhyming words.

Before Reading

Take a picture walk through the book. Stop on every page and talk about the objects on the page. Discuss what students think is happening in this story. Students may recognize the bunny's technique as one that they use to avoid going to sleep until they, like the bunny, cannot keep their eyes open!

During Reading

Read the book and enjoy the story. Then, reread the story. After you read each page, ask students to point out objects mentioned in the text. "Where is the balloon?" This is good vocabulary development for students as they learn the names of objects that may be found in their own homes. Read the story a third time and talk about the rhyming words.

Encourage Students to Join in the Reading

On the fourth reading, have students share the reading by saying the rhyming words.

Teacher:	"The cow jumping over the—"
Students:	"moon."
Teacher:	"And there were three little bears sitting on—"
Students:	"chairs."
Teacher:	"And two little kittens and a pair of—"
Students:	"mittens."

The pictures will help students finish each sentence, but they must also think of what words rhyme. For the page on which there are socks and mittens, ask, "Why didn't you say **socks**?" Students should answer that **socks** does not rhyme. You may want to have students read this story with you more than once. Let them try to read along now that they know the story. The pictures and rhymes on the pages will help many students accomplish this.

Give students a purpose to listen or read for each time. Remember to tell them what they will do after reading.

- "Listen as I read this story the first time to see if we were right when we predicted that the little bunny is trying to avoid going to bed. After I read it, we will talk about that."

- "Listen as I read the book again for all of the objects to which the bunny says good night. We will make a list of those objects after we read the book together."

- "This time as we read the story, listen for rhyming words. We will talk about the words that rhyme after we read the story."

- "Today when we read this book, I will stop at certain points. Each time I stop, I want you to say the rhyming word. The picture will help you read your part."

After Reading

Each day you read the story, have a before-, during-, and after-reading activity. One day, talk about your prediction and discuss the story. Another day, make a list of all of the things to which the bunny says good night. Following the next reading, find the rhyming words and talk about them. Another day, ask, "What do you notice?"

Open to a two-page spread in the middle of the book and ask students what they notice about the words on these pages. The lines on the pages are:

Goodnight light
And the red balloon
Goodnight bears
Goodnight chairs

Goodnight kittens
And goodnight mittens

Students say things like the following:

"There are a lot of **good nights**!"

"**Kittens** and **mittens** rhyme."

"I see the word **red**."

"**Bears** and **chairs** rhyme but do not look alike."

"**Bears** and **balloon** start with **b**."

Follow up this story with a predictable chart. Ask each child for a "Goodnight . . ." line that she would use at bedtime. *Goodnight Moon* has endless possibilities. It is a great story for shared reading at this time of year when students may have trouble going to sleep because they are anticipating the holidays.

Writing for Students

Morning Message and Journal Entry at the End of the Day

In December, write a Morning Message or a journal entry at the end of each day. This will help students keep track of what happens and what they learn each day. Writing will remind students of upcoming events and things that they need to bring to school. As you write, tell students what you are doing and why. Ask questions such as: "What letter do I need to write at the beginning of the word **Hanukkah**? What have we learned about Hanukkah? What sounds do you hear in **Hanukkah**? Let's stretch it out and listen."

Students need to know how people think as they write. They also need to know that what they say, they can also write. This knowledge will help students when they are in the Writing Center and when you ask them to write later in the year.

Morning Message

So many things happen each day during December. Write a Morning Message to tell students about the school day and after-school events. Many teachers write the Morning Message as a part of The Opening. Other teachers do it when they call the big group together for Shared Reading.

Here are some examples of December Morning Messages:

Dear Class, Today is Monday, December 7. I have a new book to read today. It is all about Hanukkah. Love, Mrs. Hall	Dear Class, Yesterday, we read a new book. What was it about? What did you learn? Love, Mrs. Hall	Dear Class, Today, we will make ornaments. We will decorate a Christmas tree with them. Love, Mrs. Hall

Each day, write a Morning Message to your class while students watch you write. Read the message with students and talk about what it says and what will happen that day. Finally, have students count the number of words and letters in each sentence.

From these experiences, students will learn the **jargon** of print. Print jargon includes terms such as **word**, **letter**, **sentence**, and **sound**. Now, this jargon also includes **message**, **greeting**, and **closing**.

Writing with Students

Predictable Charts

After discussing the holidays in December, begin writing a predictable chart on a large piece of paper. A predictable chart that students love to write during this season is titled *For the Holidays* and includes the repeating sentence "I want . . . ." Each student tells one thing that she wants or wants to do most during the holiday season. When writing the student's response, include her name in parentheses after the sentence. Dictating the sentences takes a day or two, depending on the class size.

For the Holidays

I want a basketball. (Jay)

I want a teddy bear. (Jessica)

I want a doll. (Carmen)

I want a computer. (Raul)

I want a book. (Adam S.)

I want a Panthers jacket. (Adam J.)

I want a video game. (Sierra)

I want a bike. (Marla)

I want to go sledding. (Danielle)

I want to see my Grandma. (Camden)

I want to visit my Nana and Grandpa. (Ross)

I want a toy airplane. (Hayden)

I want to play with my cousin. (Torika)

I want peace in the world. (Jacoby)

Touch Reading and What Do You Notice?

On the next day, students reread the holiday predictable chart. Each student reads his own sentence, touching each word as he reads it. Then, ask students to look at the sentences and point out what they notice about them. Students will notice a variety of things depending on their levels of development. Things they may notice include the following:

"All sentences begin with **I want**."

"**I** is always a capital letter!"

"**Basketball**, **book**, **bear**, and **bike** begin with **b**."

"**Raul** and **Ross** start with **R**."

"A lot of students want toys."

"All sentences have periods at the ends."

Accept and praise whatever students notice. Ask more questions, such as: "Can anyone find any other words that begin with **r**? Why is there a period at the end of each sentence?"

Sentence Builders

On the fourth day, write the first sentence from the chart on a sentence strip with a thick black marker. Have a child find the sentence on the chart and match the sentence strip to it. Next, have students watch as you cut the sentence into words. Mix up the words and let students become the sentence builders. Give each child a word. Include the child whose sentence is being built and give her her name. Ask students to stand in front of the class in order so that they look like the sentence on the chart. Some students will check the chart and get in their places. Others will not only find their places quickly, but they will also help anyone who does not get in the right place. Read the sentence aloud after students get in place so that other students can check to see if the sentence is correct. Repeat this procedure for each sentence on the chart.

Making a Class Book

On the fifth day, students reread the predictable chart. Write each sentence on a sentence strip, cut the sentences into words, and give each student his own sentence. Let each child arrange his sentence on a piece of paper. After you check the sentences, students can paste the words on the paper. Next, students can illustrate their sentences.

Then, put the pages together in a class big book. Read the class book aloud before adding it to the Reading Center.

Developing Phonemic Awareness

Rhyming Books

A favorite rhyming story at this time of year is *'Twas the Night Before Christmas* by Clement C. Moore (public domain). After reading the story several times, have students listen for the rhyming words. Students can jingle a bell each time they hear a rhyming word! Or, perhaps you can read the story, leave out the rhyming words, and see if students can figure out what the words are.

Teacher: "'Twas the night before Christmas, when all through the house
Not a creature was stirring, not even a— "
Students: "mouse;"
Teacher: "The stockings were hung by the chimney with care,
In hopes that Saint Nicholas soon would be—"
Students: "there;"
Teacher: "The children were nestled all snug in their beds,
while visions of sugar-plums danced in their—"
Students: "heads;"

There are many holiday songs, stories, and fingerplays that will help students learn about rhyming words. Take the opportunity to point out the rhyming words as students enjoy these activities.

Centers

Reading Center

The Reading Center is filled with books about the winter holidays that people celebrate in the United States, Canada, and other countries. Many students are trying to read *'Twas the Night Before Christmas* because they have heard it so many times. They can predict what is coming next in the story and use the pictures and the letters at the beginnings of words to figure out the text. **This is a good time to add catalogs to the Reading Center.** Students quickly learn how to find what they are wishing for in these books that are full of pictures and print. Catalogs are plentiful at holiday time, but if you do not have enough to bring to school for the Reading Center, ask parents to donate.

Writing Center

The Writing Center is filled with holiday words and pictures. The crayons, markers, pencils, pens, and stamps are familiar to students by this time of year. Some students are ready to make December Picture Dictionaries. Others are trying to write letters to Santa using pictures and what they know about print. Students have plenty to say, and they now know that they can write their holiday wishes to make sure that the right people know what they want! Holiday cards are also fun to make in the Writing Center. Provide card stock or heavy paper and envelopes. Holiday stickers, stamps, and old cards can be used to make new cards. Familiar greetings can be copied from sentence-strip signs: *Happy Holidays! Season's Greetings! Merry Christmas! Happy Hanukkah! Happy Kwanzaa!*

January

In many parts of the United States and Canada, January is a cold and snowy month, while in other areas, it is mild. Regardless of the weather where students live, they can learn about snow, cold weather, and winter activities by reading books. Reading is a way for students to slide down snow-covered hills, make a snowman with family or friends, and slide or glide on ice. It is a way see how and why people bundle up to keep warm when the temperature drops. Students can also learn how animals and birds survive these cold winter days. Students can learn about winter from reading both fiction and nonfiction (informational) books.

The Opening

The Opening continues with the calendar. It is not only a new month, but it is also a new year. Students are familiar with the days of the week and the date, but they have a new concept to work on—the order of the months, beginning with January. *Chicken Soup with Rice: A Book of Months* by Maurice Sendak (HarperTrophy, 1962) is a good book to read at this time. It takes students through the year, month by month, and it does it in rhyme! Talk about the months and how each is different from the others. Talk about the rhymes in the book as well. Can most students hear the rhymes now? Read *Chicken Soup with Rice* twice; it is mighty nice!

This month is an interesting time to watch the thermometer and see how often it goes below freezing in your area. The Opening is a good time to graph the temperature each day and to talk about types of weather: sunny, cloudy, windy, rainy, or snowy. The Morning Message may be weather-related or tell about special plans for the day.

> Dear Class,
>
> Yesterday, we made a snowman.
>
> Today, we will bring him inside.
>
> What will happen to him?
>
> Watch and see!
>
> Love,
>
> Mrs. Hall

Talk as you write, thinking aloud about what you are writing and why. Stretch out words, like **yesterday** and **happen**, so that students can see how adults spell words about which they are unsure. Let students spell many words for you—especially the high-frequency words that they know: **we**, **to**, **will**, **a**, **and**, **see**, etc.

The routine of The Opening does not change, but the subjects and the weather do! There is a lot for students to think, talk, and learn about during The Opening. **As the year progresses, the amount of learning expected of these students grows as their knowledge of the world and words grows.**

Reading Aloud to Students

Winter in many places means cold days, early nights, and a lot of time to cuddle up with good books. For students who live in areas without snow, it is a time to find out what happens in colder climates. There are many stories about winter and informational books about winter and what animals do in winter that can be read this month.

Favorite Winter Stories to Read in January

Animals in Winter by Henrietta Bancroft and Richard G. Van Gelder (HarperTrophy, 1996)

Bear Snores On by Karma Wilson (Margaret K. McElderry, 2002)

A Busy Year by Leo Lionni (Scholastic, 1993)

Calendar by Myra Cohn Livingston (Holiday House, 2007)

A Child's Year by Joan Walsh Anglund (Golden Books, 1992)

First Snow by Emily Arnold McCully (HarperCollins, 1985)

Hello, Snow! by Wendy Cheyette Lewison (Grosset & Dunlap, 1994)

Just a Snowy Vacation by Gina Mayer (Golden Books, 2001)

Katy and the Big Snow by Virginia Lee Burton (Houghton Mifflin, 1971)

Mike Mulligan and His Steam Shovel by Virginia Lee Burton (Houghton Mifflin, 1939)

The Mitten by Jan Brett (Putnam Juvenile, 1989)

The Old Man's Mitten by Yevonne Pollock (Mondo, 1994)

The 100th Day of School by Angela Shelf Medearis (Cartwheel, 1996)

Owl Moon by Jane Yolen (Philomel, 1987)

Polar Bear, Polar Bear, What Do You Hear? by Bill Martin Jr. (Puffin, 1991)

The Snowy Day by Ezra Jack Keats (Viking, 1962)

When It Snows by JoAnne Nelson (Modern Curriculum Press, 1993)

Winter: Discovering the Seasons by Louis Santrey (Troll Communications, 1983)

You Can Do It, Sam by Amy Hest (Candlewick, 2003)

Reading and Writing with Students

A favorite book to read in the winter is the Ukrainian folktale *The Mitten* by Jan Brett (Putnam Juvenile, 1989). In this version of the story, a boy named Nicki wants his grandmother, Baba, to knit him a pair of mittens as white as snow. She worries that the new mittens will be easy to lose in the snow. Sure enough, while playing outdoors, Nicki loses one of his snow-white mittens. He cannot find it in the snow, but the woodland animals do. It becomes the crowded home of a mole, a rabbit, a hedgehog, an owl, a badger, a fox, a bear, and even a tiny mouse! When the mouse tickles the bear's nose, the bear sneezes, scattering the animals and sending the mitten up in the air, where Nicki catches it. At the end of the story, Baba is happy to see Nicki safe at home with both of his mittens.

Shared Reading

You may want to read this story several times, but you may want to read different versions. First, read and talk about the story, discussing both the winter scenery and the animals. Are they familiar animals? Local animals? Big or small animals? Could they fit inside the mitten? Read the story again and list the animals you meet, in order, on a piece of chart paper or on the board. The next day, read another version of the story and discuss it. How is it the same or different? Reread the story and list the animals in this version on the same piece of chart paper or next to the first list of animals on the board. Repeat this procedure for any versions of the book you have, including the big book version. Compare the versions. Let students join you for shared reading of this story, especially with the predictable versions.

Shared Writing

Finally, have students write the story with you in a shared-writing format. Lead the discussion and let students say sentences about the story and what happens to the mitten. The story should now be predictable.

- The grandmother makes a pair of mittens for the boy. Do they have to be white?

- The boy goes outside and drops one mitten.

- Who finds the mitten? You will have to decide which animals you will include in your version.

- How does the story end? Since there are several endings, decide if the class wants the mitten to end up whole or in pieces.

- Is this story real or make-believe? Could each of the animals fit inside a mitten?

As you write the chart, talk about what you are writing and why. Ask students for help with both the composition and the spelling so that they learn how to think while writing.

Here is a sample story written by a kindergarten class:

The Mitten

A boy wanted a pair of mittens.

His Grandma made him some new mittens.

He went out to play in the snow.

He lost a mitten.

A rabbit went in the mitten.

An owl went in the mitten.

A frog went in the mitten.

A fox went in the mitten.

A bear went in the mitten.

A mouse went in the mitten.

The bear sneezed, and out came the animals.

The boy was happy because he found his mitten.

Making Their Own Books

Write the first sentence from the class's version of the story on a piece of paper, draw a box around each word, and duplicate this paper for each student. Have students cut apart the sentences and paste the words in the correct order on construction paper. Some teachers cut the construction paper in the shape of a mitten! Let students illustrate the sentence. This will be the first page of each student's book. Follow the same procedure for pages two through twelve.

When all pages of the book are complete, make a cover for each student's book and staple the cover and pages together. Write the name of the book and the student's name on the cover. Students can then take home their versions of *The Mitten* to read to their families and friends. It is interesting to see how many students can really read their versions and how many are pretend reading at this time.

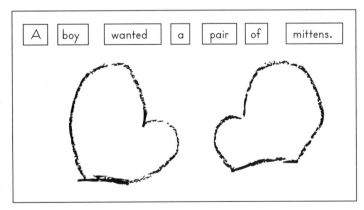

Reading by Students

Self-Selected Reading

After your daily read-aloud time, let the entire class read for a few minutes. A good way to get ready for this activity is to prepare four or five book buckets. These are usually dish pans filled with familiar books that have been read to the class; easy, predictable beginning readers; old favorites, like Dr. Seuss books; and books on the current theme. This time is called Self-Selected Reading because students can choose the books they want to read from the buckets and there is no follow-up activity. In addition to the books in the book buckets, let students choose from class-made big books, children's magazines, and magazines brought from home.

- After having students choose reading materials, let students sit in their seats or find comfortable places in the classroom to read.

- Most kindergarten teachers begin with five minutes and later lengthen the time period for Self-Selected Reading. A kitchen timer can help make this activity easier for you. Tell students how many minutes they can spend reading today. Then, set the timer.

- Invite students to read silently until they hear the timer go off. Most students need a quiet place to read, so it is important to start with a small amount of time and encourage students to be as quiet as possible.

- Circulate around the room, visiting several students and listening to them as they each read a few lines to you.

- Talk about the books they are reading. What is happening in the stories? What do they think will happen next? Why?

- When the timer goes off, ask students to put their books back into the book buckets or in the Reading Center.

> The purpose of Self-Selected Reading is to let students have time to read each day so that reading becomes a habit. This is the time when students put into practice the strategies you have been teaching them.

Writing for Students

Morning Message

Continue writing Morning Messages about January events. Let students tell you what to say and how to write it. In the second half of kindergarten, the Morning Message should be more interactive. Let students help with ideas and writing.

Writing by Students

Journal Writing

Tell students that **the new year is a good time for students to begin writing their own journal entries**. Students have been in kindergarten for almost half of the school year, and they have watched you write on numerous occasions. You have modeled journal writing at the end of each day, you have written with students as you made predictable charts, and you have done shared writing together. Most students are now ready to begin writing on their own.

Some teachers use sheets of plain paper and a bookbinder to make a journal for each student to use during the remainder of the year. Other teachers staple together several sheets of paper each month so that students start with January journals and have new journals each month. Decide which format will work best for you and your students.

> It is usually best to use plain paper for student journals because some students are not ready to write on lined paper. If your class is multilevel (and most kindergarten classes are!), some students are ready to "drite" (draw and write) while others are ready to write words or a few sentences. The first day you ask students to write in their journals, it is a good idea to do a lesson reminding them of the ways people write.

Just like you did at the beginning of the year, tell students that some people use pictures when they write. Draw a smiling face on the board to illustrate this.

"When you see this face, you know that someone is happy or likes what she is doing. If someone wrote **I** and drew a smiling face and a piece of pizza, what would she be saying?"

"Yes, she would be saying that she likes pizza!"

Next, draw some wavy lines.

"Some children pretend to write when they do not know how to write or which letters to make. I did this when I was little, and I thought that I was writing like my family did. When you write in your journals, it is OK to pretend to write."

Then, write a few words that students might know:

dog

love

Miss Williams

"Some people use words that they know to write messages. You know that this says **dog**, this says **love**, and this is my name, **Miss Williams**."

Write a few simple sentences on the board:

I love you.

I love my dog.

While you are writing, say something like the following:

"Some of you may be able to use words and sentences when writing in your journals—just like I do. Sometimes, we are not sure what letters are in the words that we want to write, so we stretch out the words, listen for the sounds, and write the letters that make those sounds."

Stretch out some of the words you have written on the board so that your students can see you write each letter as they hear the sound (l–o–v–e, d–o–g, p–i–z–z–a).

At the conclusion of your mini-lesson, tell students that when they write in their journals, they can draw, write, or do both.

Encouraging students to stretch out words and listen to the sounds helps them develop phonemic awareness. Writing the letters for the sounds that students hear helps them use the phonics they know.

As students try to spell words, they should do the following:

- **Say the word slowly, stretching it out.**
- **Listen to themselves saying the sounds.**
- **Think about what they have learned about letters and sounds.**
- **Write the letters for the sounds they hear.**

The next day, model drawing a picture and writing a sentence. Draw a simple picture of you reading a book and write **I like to read**. Then, ask students to do the same. Let each student use a page in his journal to "drite." Every day this month, model drawing a simple picture and writing a simple sentence. Writing daily gives students opportunities to use their knowledge of letters, sounds, and words. It is wonderful to see young students writing what they want to say by slowly saying words and listening for the letter sounds they know.

Phonemic Awareness/Phonics

In addition to encouraging students to write the sounds that they hear (**sound spelling/spelling by ear/invented spelling/temporary spelling/phonics spelling**), there are other activities that help students develop phonemic awareness.

Rhyming Books

Continue to read books that have some rhyming words, such as *Eeny, Meeny, Miney Mouse* by Gwen Pascoe (Educational Insights, 1987). As always, the first reading of this book is for enjoyment. The second time you read the book to the class, ask students to listen for the rhyming words. Talk about the words that rhyme on each page:

mouse/house   moo/shoe   mole/whole   mums/crumbs   munch/lunch   mat/cat

If students are still having trouble hearing rhymes, stop there. If they can hear the rhyming words easily, write the words on the board or write them on index cards and put them in a pocket chart. Next, underline the rhyming or spelling patterns in the words so that students can see them:

m<u>ouse</u>	m<u>oo</u>	m<u>ole</u>	m<u>ums</u>	m<u>unch</u>	m<u>at</u>
h<u>ouse</u>	sh<u>oe</u>	wh<u>ole</u>	cr<u>umbs</u>	l<u>unch</u>	c<u>at</u>

Call attention to the spelling patterns in these words that are the same. Cross off the patterns that are not the same. Let students know that words that rhyme often have the same spelling pattern, but not always. If the words do have the same spelling pattern, you can use the pattern to read and write other words.

Point to **munch** and **lunch**. Then, write **bunch** and **crunch**.

Point to **mat** and **cat**. Then, write **hat** and **flat**.

Clapping Syllables

An activity that may help students listen to words and separate them into beats is clapping syllables. You can do this with the animal names in *The Mitten* (see Reading and Writing with Students, pages 74–75).

- Write **owl**, **rabbit**, **mole**, **fox**, **hedgehog**, and **bear** on index cards for a pocket chart or on the board.

- Tell students that you will say the animal names and they should listen for the beats in each animal name.

- Ask students to clap to show how many beats each word has.

- Say each animal name one at a time.

- Help students decide that **owl** is a one-clap, one-beat word and that **rabbit** takes two claps and is a two-beat word.

Once you have said all six words, do the exercise again, showing the words to students as they clap the beats. **Explain that if a word has more claps, it probably has more letters.** How many claps are in the word **animal**?

Making Words

You can also work on phonemic awareness with students by doing a Making Words activity. To prepare for each lesson, write each letter needed on a sheet of white construction paper with a thick black marker. Then, laminate the sheets so that they may be saved and reused. Punch a hole at the top of each side of each sheet of paper and tie lengths of yarn through the holes. Each piece of yarn should be long enough to hang around a student's neck. Instead, you may wish to purchase yellow vinyl letter vests from a school supply store or a catalog. These vests usually have a lowercase letter on one side and the corresponding uppercase letter on the other side.

First, read a book like *The Cat in the Hat* by Dr. Seuss (Random House, 1957), *Cats* by Helen Frost (Capstone Press, 2001), or *I Love Cats* by Barney Saltzberg (Candlewick, 2005). Then, choose two students to become the **at** spelling pattern: one student wears the **a** card and one student wears the **t** card. Have the students stand together at the front of the classroom. Blend together the letter sounds: **a–t**. Have eight other students become the letters **b, c, h, f, m, p, s,** and **r**. Have students with the letters that spell **c–a–t** stand together at the front of the classroom. Say the letters **c, a,** and **t** and say the word **cat**. Take away the **c** by having the **c** student stand to the side. Read aloud what is left: **at**. Then, one at a time, have each student wearing a letter stand next to **at**. Blend the letter sound with **at**. See who can read each new word as each student who is wearing a letter card joins **at** (**mat, pat,** etc.). This manipulation of letters—blending and segmenting letters and sounds to make new words—is an important part of learning how to read.

To end this lesson, ask students to help you spell some words. Ask, "What letter is needed to spell **cat**?" Tell students to point to the student wearing the letter, and have the **c** student stand next to the **a** and **t** students. Help students spell **c–a–t** and say **cat**. Do this for the letters needed to spell **bat, fat, hat, mat, pat, rat,** and **sat**.

Other spelling patterns to use for Making Words lessons this month are **am**, **ad**, **ap**, and **an**.

Making Words Lessons

For each lesson, do the following:

1. Read a book with the selected pattern in the title and/or in the book.

2. Make and read words with the pattern.

3. Decide what letters to use with the pattern to spell some words. Have students point to each needed letter and have the student with that letter join the other letter students.

Here are letters, books, and words needed for each pattern this month:

Pattern: am

Letters: a m b h j P r S t w

Books to Read:

Bread and Jam for Frances by Russell Hoban (HarperTrophy, 1993)

Green Eggs and Ham by Dr. Seuss (Random House, 1960)

Words to Read and Spell: bam, ham, jam, Pam, ram, Sam, tam, wham

Pattern: ad

Letters: a d b C d f h l m p s

Book to Read:

I Can Read with My Eyes Shut! by Dr. Seuss (Random House, 1978)

Read the book. Reread pages 22–23 and talk about the **ad** pattern in **sad**, **glad**, and **mad**.

Words to Read and Spell: bad, dad, fad, had, lad, mad, pad, sad, Chad

Pattern: ap

Letters: a p c g m n r t z

Books to Read:

Caps for Sale: A Tale of a Peddler, Some Monkeys and Their Monkey Business by Esphyr Slobodkina (HarperTrophy, 1940)

Any book about maps

Words to Read and Spell: cap, gap, lap, map, nap, rap, tap, zap

Pattern: an

Letters: a n c D f m p r s t v

Book to Read:

The Gingerbread Man, any version

Words to Read and Spell: can, Dan, fan, man, pan, ran, tan, van, scan

Centers

Reading Center

The Reading Center is filled with books that students have heard in class and can now read and pretend read on their own. Students can also read many class books that they helped make. It is now time to add books with snow pictures to the Reading Center. This is also a good time to read about and discuss snowmen, sleds, skates, and snowplows. Students like to read winter books even if they don't have winter weather.

Writing Center

The Writing Center has new words posted for a January Picture Dictionary. Students can decorate paper with snowmen and snow scenes. If you have a computer in your classroom, talk about how students can write on computers. A computer can make writing much easier for students who have difficulty with handwriting.

Assessing Progress

Assessment is an ongoing process for experienced kindergarten teachers who have become good student watchers.

- As students respond to various activities, notice who can do what. If you write what you notice, you will have anecdotal records!

- Samples—particularly writing samples—are also informative. By comparing early and later samples of a student's work, growth can be determined and validated.

In kindergarten, most teachers want to do individual student assessments. What you assess and how you do it should mirror your instruction. Some tasks that will help you assess the concepts on which you have been concentrating are included in this chapter. Some students will be able to complete all of these tasks successfully. Hopefully, every child will be able to do at least some of the tasks. Before you begin your assessment, make sure that you have all of the necessary materials. Then, decide when you will do the assessment and how many students you will assess each day. **Assessment should not take too long; try to finish assessing your entire class in one week. Center time is usually a good time to do individual assessments.**

Here are some things you should assess at this point of kindergarten:

Assessing Words

Students who are progressing should have learned some words used in daily activities, including the names of their classmates and words used in The Opening. Most students will not have learned all of their classmate's names or all of The Opening words, but some students will have learned all of them. To assess word learning, write the first names of students on index cards. Put them in a pocket chart or spread them out on the table. Ask each child to choose three to five name cards and read them to you. **Students who can read three to five names are making progress with word learning.** Some students will want to and be able to read more names.

Do a similar activity with words used in The Opening. Write some words that you use each day during The Opening, including the **days of the week and weather words**. Ask each child to read the names of three to five days of the week and three weather words (**sunny, cloudy, rainy**).

Assessing Letter Names

You have been talking about letters and letter names during The Opening, when working with students' names, when writing, when reading big books, and when asking, "What do you notice?" **It is now time to see if students recognize some letter names.** It is not necessary for students to know all 52 uppercase and lowercase letters at this time, but they should have learned some of them. Make copies of page 64 or write six unconfusing capital letters (**A**, **D**, **B**, **M**, **S**, and **R**) and six lowercase letters (**o**, **i**, **e**, **c**, **t**, and **n**) separately on index cards. **Ask each student to pick up and name as many letters as she can.** If this task seems easy for many students, add more letters.

Assessing Phonemic Awareness

You have been clapping the syllables in students' names and working with the concept of rhyme. Find out if students are progressing in these two areas of phonemic awareness.

Choose several students' names, each with a different number of syllables. Ask each child to say each name and clap the beats. For example, if you said **Jasmine**, the student would repeat the name and clap twice. The child would also clap twice for **Ryan**. For **Paul**, the child would clap once.

To assess rhyme, make copies of page 63 or collect six pictures of common objects that have rhyming names.

bike   bed   cat   cake   van   bus

Name the six pictures with the child. Then, have the child name them. Next, tell the child that you will say a name and he should repeat the name and find a picture that rhymes with it. Do one together as an example:

"The first name is **Ted**. Say **Ted** and the names of the pictures. Which picture name rhymes with **Ted**?"

Help the child realize that **Ted** and **bed** rhyme. Have the child say *"Ted–bed"* several times and remove the bed picture. Now, there are five pictures left.

Name each picture and have the child repeat each name and find the picture that rhymes with each of the following names:

    Mike   Pat   Jake   Dan   Gus

To assess beginning sounds, have each student listen to two words and ask her if the words begin alike. Say the following pairs:

Billy, birthday	Jasmine, jump	bike, ball	Chad, cherries	cat, cup
Billy, cake	Jasmine, walk	bike, magic	Chad, bananas	cat, dog

Assessing Print Concepts

Reading requires particular ways of moving the eyes and an understanding of jargon, such as **word**, **letter**, etc. Often, students who do not come from literacy-rich homes are confused by the jargon. Although students speak in words, they do not know that words exist as separate entities until they start reading and writing at school. **To many students, *letters* are what you get in the mailbox; *sounds* are horns, bells, and slamming doors; and *a sentence* is what a person serves if she commits a crime!** These students may be unable to follow your instructions because you are using words that, for them, either have no meaning or have different meanings. All year, you have helped students develop the concepts and jargon of print that they need to progress in reading. Now, it is time to assess how their print concepts are developing.

For this assessment, use a predictable book that was used for shared reading or use a class big book that you created from a predictable chart. **First, ask a student to show you the front of the book. Turn to the first page and ask her to point to where she would start to read. Then, have her point to words for you to read them. Notice if she is pointing to just one word at a time and making the correct return sweep.**

Next, ask her to **point to just one word anywhere on the page**. Then, **have her point to the first word on the page, then the last word on the page**. Ask her to **point to just one letter anywhere on the page**. Then, pick a word from the page and **ask her to point to the first letter of the word and the last letter of the word**.

Using Assessment Results

Use the Kindergarten Assessment Checklist (page 62) or create your own. Analyze the progress of each child. On a class summary sheet, list students who do not seem to be progressing as quickly as they should. Put this sheet in a place where you will see it often and use it as a reminder for whom to focus on during activities for the upcoming month. While reading big books or predictable charts, ask students who still cannot track print to be pointers during the activity. Help these students show just one word, the last word in the sentence, and so on. Likewise, during the Morning Message and other activities with words, move students who need work with word learning and letter-name knowledge closer to you and call on them more often. Provide individual coaching and nudges to these students as you work with the class. Ask students whose syllable-clapping and rhyming responses indicate difficulty in developing phonemic awareness to lead rhyming and clapping activities with you. Also, work individually or in a small group with students who still need additional time and practice by rereading big books or charts and by focusing on these concepts, especially during center time. At the end of next month, reassess students about whose progress you are concerned, concentrating on the concepts with which the students had problems.

February

February is another cold winter month in many places. Some schools have winter vacations so that everyone can enjoy the snow and winter activities. In other places, snow may mean no school, and activities come to a stop. What happens at your school depends on the area in which you live, but no matter where you live, snow fascinates young students.

The Opening

The Opening continues with the same routine that was established months ago. **Young students thrive on routine because they know what to do and when to do it.** Students answer questions and look at the words that have now become familiar to them—the days of the week, the months, and weather words. Since these words are already familiar to students, use them to teach more about letter-sound correspondence.

Teacher: "How do we know that this word is **Wednesday**?"

Student: "It begins with **W**."

Teacher: "How do you know that it isn't **Tuesday**?"

Student: "It does not have **T** at the beginning."

Teacher: "What is the weather like today?"

Student: "Cold and cloudy."

Teacher: "Who can point to the word **cold**?"

Student: (Points to the word **cold** on the bulletin board.)

Teacher: "Who can point to the word **cloudy**?"

Student: (Points to the word **cloudy** on the bulletin board.)

Teacher: "How do you know that that word is **cloudy**?"

Student: "It begins with **cl**. "

If the student answers that **cloudy** begins with **c**, point out that **cold** begins with **c** as well. Then, say, "Listen to the word **cloudy**." (Stretch out **cloudy** so that students can hear the two sounds blended together at the beginning. "What two letters do you hear at the beginning of **cloudy**?"

If students have been counting the days of school by bundling together straws, **it should be almost time to celebrate 100 days of school**. This usually happens in February. The 10 tens now go into a bigger bundle so that students can see what 100 straws look like. Some teachers ask students to bring in other sets of hundreds—100 pennies, 100 pieces of candy, 100 paper clips, 100 raisins, etc.— and display these in the classroom. **Kindergarten students have reached a milestone in school: 100 days of literacy and learning!**

There is still time to read winter stories that students love even if you do not live where it gets cold enough to snow. February is a good time to talk about what happens to birds, animals, plants, and people in winter.

Some teachers use penguins, presidents, and hibernation as February themes. As Valentine's Day approaches, love is a wonderful theme to use. Kindergarten students enjoy making hearts and valentines and reading and writing about love. Students talk about the people they love and the things they love to do. Some classes even make cookies and decorate them for a Valentine's Day party.

Reading Aloud to Students

February is a short month in which you have much to do and many books you can read. You can read books about the U.S. presidents George Washington and Abraham Lincoln and books about Groundhog Day and Valentine's Day. There are also many wonderful alphabet books that fit into February themes or units. Simple books with a few words on each page and pictures that most students recognize are the most helpful in building a student's letter-sound and letter-name knowledge. Once a book has been read and reread several times, students will enjoy reading it for themselves when they go to the Reading Center. It is very important that students have time to read books of their own choosing each day. Simple alphabet books that have been read as a class are items that students can read on their own. Easy leveled readers are also especially well suited for kindergarten students to read at Self-Selected Reading time. If you want students to choose these easy-to-read books, you must read them aloud. According to Linda Gambrell, the 2007–2008 president of the International Reading Association, teachers "bless" books when they read them to the class, and students want to read these books when they are reading by themselves.

Some books to read in February include the following:

Arthur's Valentine by Marc Brown (Little, Brown Young Readers, 1980)

The Best Thing About Valentines by Eleanor Hudson (Cartwheel, 2004)

The Biggest Valentine Ever by Steven Kroll (Cartwheel, 2006)

Clifford's First Valentine's Day by Norman Bridwell (Cartwheel, 1997)

Franklin's Valentine's Day by Paulette Bourgeois (Scholastic, 1999)

Gretchen Groundhog It's Your Day by Abby Levine (Albert Whitman & Company, 1998)

Guess How Much I Love You by Sam McBratney (Candlewick, 1994)

The Happy Hedgehog by Marcus Pfister (North-South Books, 2000)

Lilly's Chocolate Heart by Kevin Henkes (HarperCollins, 2003)

February

The Night Before Valentine's Day by Natasha Wing (Grosset & Dunlap, 2001)

You're All My Favorites by Sam McBratney (Candlewick, 2004)

Alphabet Books

Some alphabet books to read in February that meet the "not too many words, familiar pictures, and students love to read them" criteria include the following:

A My Name Is Alice by Jane Bayer (Puffin, 1984)

A You're Adorable by Buddy Kaye, Fred Wise, and Sidney Lippman (Candlewick, 1996)

The Accidental Zucchini: An Unexpected Alphabet by Max Grover (Voyager Books, 1993)

All Aboard ABC by Douglas Magee and Robert Newman (Puffin, 1990)

Alphabatics by Suse MacDonald (Aladdin, 1986)

Alphabet City by Stephen T. Johnson (Puffin, 1995)

The Alphabet Tale by Jan Garten (Greenwillow, 1994)

Animal ABCs by Susan Hood (Troll Communications, 1997)

Dr. Seuss's ABC by Dr. Seuss (Random House, 1963)

Eating the Alphabet: Fruits and Vegetables from A to Z by Lois Ehlert (Harcourt, 1989)

From Acorn to Zoo and Everything in Between in Alphabetical Order by Satoshi Kitamusa (Farrar, Straus and Giroux, 1992)

It Begins with an A by Stephanie Calmenson (Hyperion, 1994)

K Is for Kiss Good Night: A Bedtime Alphabet by Jill Sardegna (Random House, 1994)

On Market Street by Arnold Lobel (HarperTrophy, 1964)

Sleepy ABC by Margaret Wise Brown (HarperCollins, 1994)

Reading with Students

Shared Reading with Predictable Big Books

The school year is now halfway over. February is a good time to consolidate what students know about letters and sounds. There are many big-book alphabet books, including big book dictionaries, that you can use. Big-book alphabet books to use in kindergarten are *From Acorn to Zoo and Everything in Between in Alphabetical Order* by Satoshi Kitamusa (Farrar, Straus and Giroux, 1992), *My Picture Dictionary* by Diane Snowball and Robyn Greene (Mondo, 1994), and *ABC and You* by Eugenie Fernandes (Penguin Putnam, 1990). Use these alphabet dictionaries this month to talk about letters, sounds, and words.

From Acorn to Zoo and Everything in Between in Alphabetical Order can be used for shared reading. A letter and 15–20 words that begin with that letter are on each page. At the bottom of each page is a question, such as, "What is the armadillo balancing on his nose?" The answer to the question can be found in the list of words on that page—**apple**, **apricot**, **almond**, **acorn**, etc. The second time you read the book, point to each picture and have students read the pictures and answer the question at the bottom of each page. By looking at the picture on each page, students can find the answer to each question. Kindergartners like to share the work of finding the answers to the questions as they look at the pictures and think of words that match the print (same letter, same sound, same size, etc.).

My Picture Dictionary has several special features. Each page includes simple pictures and print for the letter. On the side of the page, the alphabet is listed with a character to indicate the beginning letter for the words on that page. This book is available in big-book format for whole-class modeling, as well as hardcover and paperback small-book formats. Kindergarten students also enjoy reading these dictionaries in the Reading Center. Pairs of students can read the dictionaries, with one student acting as the teacher and asking questions and the other student acting as the student and answering the questions. The pictures help students who cannot read all of the words.

ABC and You is another alphabet big book. Students find it easy to share the reading once they know that it starts with *Amazing Amanda* and ends with *Zippy Zack*. It's fun to make your own *ABC and You* predictable chart. Whose name begins with **A**? **B**? **C**? Your predictable chart can begin with *Amazing Allie* or *Adorable Adam* and continue with *Jumping Jasmine* and *Marvelous Mike* until you get to *Wonderful William* and *Zany Zoey*. This chart will help students focus on their names and think of other words that begin with the same letters and sounds. Some letters will have more than one student's name. Others will not have a name unless you introduce names for the missing letters.

After reading several alphabet books, it is fun for students to make their own. One way to do this is to have each student make a page for his book every time you begin a new letter. This project will most likely not be completed in one month because there are 26 pages and a book cover to make.

Remember that each lesson should have before-, during-, and after-reading activities.

Before Reading
Take a picture walk. Let students name the pictures on each page and find the word(s). Then, before turning the page, let students predict what letter will be on the next page.

During Reading
Do shared reading of each page.

After Reading
Talk about other things that could go on the letter pages. Make a class alphabet book (see page 92).

Writing for Students

Morning Message
The Opening is the time to talk about what will happen each day. Write a Morning Message for students telling them about the day's events. Although the concept of the Morning Message is not new, the content of each message is new and students are excited about reading the message each day. When you write **Dear Class**, it is now familiar to students. From repetition, they know that the Morning Message starts this way and so does a letter or note. Each sentence should be on a separate line until students have a good concept of what a sentence is. Then, begin to wrap the sentences around. "How many sentences are there?" is a harder question but needs to be asked so that students can learn that every line is not a sentence.

Dear Class,
Today, we will make valentines.
We will write "I love you" inside.
What will you draw on your card?
Love,
Mrs. Hall

Dear Class,
Today, we will walk to the post office to buy stamps.
Then, we will mail our valentines.
We will have fun!
Love,
Mrs. Hall

Kindergarten students know how to read and write **love** because you have signed your Morning Message this way every day. As you write your Morning Messages, let students spell **love** for you. The body of each message is always a puzzle to students, but they will look for words that they know and letters and sounds that they can figure out until some students (with a little help from you) have decoded the day's event.

Writing with Students

Predictable Charts

There are many alphabet books from which you can make predictable charts. After reading an alphabet book during Shared reading, begin a predictable chart by writing the first sentence:

A is for apple. (Miss Williams)

Students know what letter comes next, and they raise their hands because they are ready to contribute.

Sometimes, the class is not large enough to have a student response for every letter, so for the last few letters, write sentences together. Rereading the chart is fun for students because they see their names in print and can read their own sentences.

Touch Reading

On the following day, have each student touch read her sentence by touching each word as she reads it. By doing this, you can see if the student is tracking print and developing voice-to-print match.

A is for apple. (Miss Williams)
B is for bee. (Suzanne)
C is for cat. (Jasmine)
D is for dog. (Ryan)
E is for elephant. (Michelle)
F is for fish. (Paul)
G is for girl. (Grant)
H is for hat. (Nikki)
I is for ice cream. (Rayshawn)
J is for jam. (Emily)
K is for kids. (Mitchell)
L is for love. (Olivia)
M is for monkey. (Adam)
N is for nuts. (Refugio)
O is for orange. (William)
P is for pie. (Erica)
Q is for quiet. (Mike)
R is for rope. (Jacob)
S is for snake. (Jimmy)
T is for towel. (Julie)
U is for umbrella. (Tiara)
V is for valentine. (Marie)
W is for window. (Pat)
X is for X-ray.
Y is for yellow.
Z is for zoo.

Sentence Builders

On the next day, students read their sentences and become sentence builders. Choose four or five sentences from the chart, write them on sentence strips, cut them apart into words, and give each word to a different student. Beginning with the first sentence, have students come to the front of the room with their words and build the sentence by standing in order.

The first five students, including Suzanne, whose sentence students are building, come to the front of the class and build the sentence **B is for bee. (Suzanne)**. With the rest of the class, read and check the sentence. The next three or four groups follow the same procedure.

Making a Class Alphabet Book

After four or five sentences have been built, it is time for each student to cut apart his sentence and put the words in order. Earlier, you cut apart the sentences for students. Now that students understand that sentences are made of words, they are ready to cut apart their own sentences. If a few students have trouble, use their sentences to demonstrate for the class how to cut apart sentences or cut apart the sentences for them.

Then, each student arranges the words in her sentence on a large piece of paper to make it look like it does on the predictable chart. Some students must look at the chart to make sure that they are right. Other students can read all of the words and do not need help. After you check to see that the words are in order, let students paste their sentences to the bottoms of their papers. Finally, each student draws a picture to illustrate her sentence. Suzanne takes crayons and draws a big yellow and black bee—including the stinger. She was stung by bees twice last summer, and she knows what bees look like! Ryan draws his dog, a dalmatian with big black spots. Olivia draws a fancy red heart for love. After illustrating their sentences, students are ready to line up in alphabetical order and put together the class book.

Miss Williams begins with the **A** page that she used to demonstrate writing a sentence on the predictable chart, cutting apart the sentence, pasting, and illustrating it. Suzanne knows that **B** is next, so she brings her sentence to the front of the room. Jasmine follows with her **cat** picture for **C**. Ryan knows that his **dog** is after **cat**. Michelle is next, and she's proud that she has the biggest picture and the longest word so far—**elephant**. She helps Paul to find his place with his **fish** picture. Students have fun getting everyone's picture in order, using the predictable chart to check themselves. When the pages are in alphabetical order, put a piece of heavy construction paper on each side for the front and back covers. Bind together the covers and pages with a bookbinder (if available) or staple them together. Then, add this class-made big book to the Reading Center. With this big book, students will have yet another opportunity to work with letters, sounds, familiar words, and names.

There are other alphabet books you can make. Once you have read and reread the book *ABC and You*, do shared writing using students' names. Write *ABC and You* on the top of a large piece of chart paper. Ask students whose names begin with **A** to write them, along with adjectives that begin with the same letter (Awesome Adam, Admirable Allie). Let students decide whose name will be next, depending on where the student's first name falls in alphabetical order. (See example chart on page 93.)

After the chart is completed, write each student's name and adjective on a sentence strip. Or, have students copy their names and adjectives on sentence strips or large pieces of paper.

As you reread the predictable chart, have students holding their phrases line up in alphabetical order by first name. The third reading may be done by students who are lined up. If you have **Michelle**, **Mike**, and **Mitchell**, you will have to help them get in the right places. You do not need to teach alphabetical order by second and third letters, but you can mention it as you put **Michelle** in front of **Mike**, and **Mike** in front of **Mitchell**. There may be one or two students who pick up on what you are doing and why, making this a multilevel activity.

Once again, students illustrate their names and adjectives and put the drawings together in alphabetical order to make a class book. Other ideas for class alphabet books include an animal alphabet (especially if your theme is animals) and a classroom object alphabet (finding an object in the classroom that begins with each letter).

ABC and You
A..... Amazing Adam!
..... Adorable Allie!
..... Affectionate Angelica!
..... Athletic Andrew!
..... Active Ashley!
B..... Beautiful Blair Macy!
..... Brave Bret!
..... Bashful Brian!
C..... Cute Cubby!
J..... Jolly Jaleel!
..... Joyous Jessica!
..... Jumping Jonathan!
K..... Kind Kylan!
L..... Lovable Lenzi!
..... Lucky Lucas!
N..... Nice Nash!
..... Noble Nathan!

Other Predictable Chart Ideas

Another easy predictable chart is *I Love . . .*, for which everyone tells someone whom they love or something that they love.

Since it is winter, a predictable chart about winter is always welcome. Students finish the predictable sentence "In winter, I . . . (go skiing, make a snowman, ride my sled, go ice-skating, play ice hockey, etc.)"

· ·

Writing by Students

Self-Selected Writing Topics

In kindergarten classes in which teachers have been writing Morning Messages, journal entries, and predictable charts with their students, there are students who are writing and enjoying it. Many students have been writing on their own in their journals and at the Writing Center. **Now, it is time to give all students a chance to select their own writing topics. We know that students write best when they write about things they know.**

Most teachers try to give students topics about which all students have prior knowledge—the themes they are studying, upcoming holidays, things that are happening at school, etc. During journal-writing time, most students begin to write stories in their journals about the things they find interesting: the basketball game they watched last night, a trip to the beach, a pet, etc. **The topics students pick should not be limited to your ideas. If you have not already done so, give students permission to write about any topics they know. Young students expand on their classmates' topics and ideas.**

Most students write "all about" stories—all about their dogs or cats, all about their families, or all they know about basketball. Once in a while, you may have a student who attempts to write fiction, usually beginning her story with "Once upon a time . . . ." In kindergarten, fiction is not as familiar as the "all about" stories and should be recognized for the writing feat that it is.

If you have been writing **for** and **with** students daily, you may notice that students are really beginning to express themselves in writing.

Modeling Adding On to a Sentence

One day, write a sentence and illustrate it. The next day, reread the sentence and tell students that you have more to say about the topic. Then, add on to it by telling more about the topic in another sentence. Do this each day so that each week you have a five-sentence piece about one topic. When you model adding on, kindergarten students begin to write more than one sentence on a topic instead of starting a new piece each day.

Here are some examples of students' writing at this time:

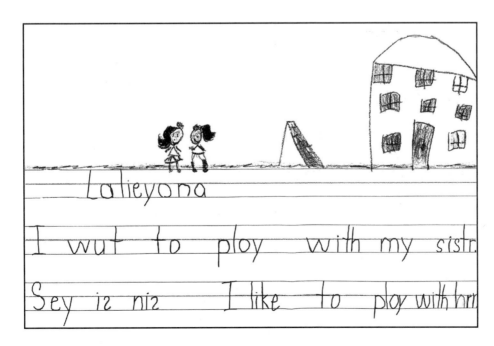

February

Rebecca has a turn on the computer and writes the following writing sample about a day in her kindergarten class. She types much more than when she writes on paper. When she writes on paper, her handwriting slows her down.

Rebecca

Daer Boys and Gruls.

I am in Mrs.Wares Class.

We Writ Storys in The Lab.

We are Good in School.

We Have Cintres Win We Get To School.

We Wolket To The Post Ofice We Got Stamps At The Post Office.

We Go On Filltrips.

We Have Lunch At 11:45.

Aftre The Silent Of Momit Bell Rings We Go To The Grop.

We Work At Cintres.

We Work Hard At Cintres.

We Do The Calindr and Wethr in The Mornin.

Most Of Us Do Ore Best Work.

We Have Snak Aftre We Come From The Lab.

Aftre Snak Mrs. Ruminsky Comes. She Hlops The Childrin She Hlops The Childrin Lron Ther Numbrs and Ther Leders.

I Rot This Not all By My Self.

Rebecca

Dear Boys and Girls.

I am in Mrs. Ware's class.

We write stories in the lab.

We are good in school.

We have centers when we get to school.

We walked to the post office. We got stamps at the post office.

We go on field trips.

We have lunch at 11:45.

After the Moment of Silence bell rings we go to the group.

We work at centers.

We work hard at centers.

We do the calendar and weather in the morning.

Most of us do our best work.

We have snack after we come from the lab.

After snack Mrs. Ruminsky comes. She helps children. She helps the children learn their numbers and their letters.

I wrote this note all by myself.

Some kindergarten students will take risks and write fiction. Do you notice the Southern accent?

> Bailey
>
> wons upon a tim a litl gol had a haond. tat nit the haond ran in to the forist. the litl gol cod not fiend hm. the litl gol was wored. the haond sol a fox. tha wr best frans. tha navr did bad thags to ej othr. tha wr bast frans for avr. the fox and the haond

Bailey
Once upon a time a little girl had a hound. That night the hound ran into the forest. The little girl could not find him. The little girl was worried. The hound saw a fox. They were best friends. They never did bad things to each other. They were best friends forever, the fox and the hound.

Note: This was written by a student whose teacher did not do Morning Messages. Although she is a good kindergarten writer, she did not start her sentences with capital letters. This usually doesn't happen if the teacher models and talks about capital letters while writing Morning Messages.

Coaching Writing and Using Invented Spelling or Phonics Spelling

How did these young students get so good at writing? They had teachers who modeled what writing is and how to think and write each day during the Morning Message and journal writing. Their teachers also took the time to coach them. Coaching means sitting down with students and helping them say what they want to write, helping them listen for the words they know how to write (words they have seen in print all year), and helping them stretch out the words they do not know by listening for the sounds they can represent with letters. When you write a student's sentence instead of having him write it, you do not find out what he actually knows about letter-sound relationships or words. When students invent words they do not know, you learn about their word knowledge and how they represent sounds in the words that they are writing. If kindergarten students are limited to writing only the words that they can spell correctly, they cannot write very much. If you write the words that students cannot spell for them, you will learn nothing about what they know about the words. If you say, "Stretch out that word and listen for the sounds you hear," then you can learn about what students know. You will learn how many phonemes students can hear and know how to represent.

> After seeing the writing samples on the previous pages, you may be thinking, "My kindergarten students can't write like that."
>
> They **can** and **will** if you believe that they can and you continue to model and coach them.

J. Richard Gentry's work can give you a better understanding of how young students learn to spell and write. Read his work on the stages of spelling (writing) development in his article in *Early Years K–8* (May 1985) titled "You Can Analyze Developmental Spelling—And Here's How to Do It!" or his two books, *Spel . . . Is a Four Letter Word* (Heinemann, 1987) and *Teaching Students to Spell* with Jean Wallace Gillet (Heinemann, 1993). Gentry writes that a teacher's awareness of students' developmental-spelling progress enables her to respond intelligently when working with students.

February

During writing time, a teacher has an opportunity to both respond to and coach students so that they can become better writers and better spellers as they learn more about words and writing. What the teacher says and does with students daily depends on the students with which he is working and what they know. Gentry's spelling stages are listed on the following pages, along with samples of student work for each stage.

Stages of Spelling Development

Stage 1: The Precommunicative or Pre-phonemic Stage

In this stage, students do not know about phonemes—letters and letter sounds. Spelling and writing contains scribbles (see Corey's work) or random letters (see Sarah, Tony, and Angelica's works).

Corey scribbles when asked to write. He uses no letters or words in his writing. Often, students use wavy lines in their attempts to imitate their parents' writing.

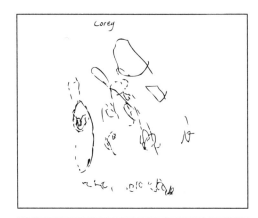

Sarah writes with random letters, "I love my mommy and I love my sister." Notice that there is no correspondence between letters and sounds in words. Sarah knows that she can use letters to represent the sounds in words; she just doesn't know which ones!

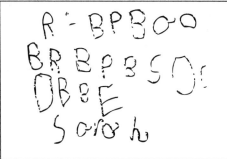

Tony writes about all of the things that he loves too. "I love Dad. I love Mom. I love basketball. I love pizza . . . ." Tony knows that there are words in sentences. (His teacher has been writing predictable charts!) He has more word knowledge than Sarah, but like Sarah, he has not figured out which letters represent which sounds.

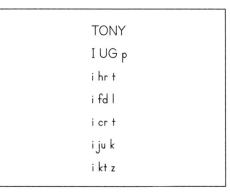

Angelica has copied the alphabet in the room. She writes some random letters (**n**'s and **o**'s) and draws pictures. Angelica copies. Students at this stage like to copy if they know that letters can represent sounds but do not know which ones.

Stage 2: The Semiphonetic Stage

The second stage can be seen when words begin to be represented by letters. The letters students write are usually the first letter in a word or the first and last letters.

Terry represents **dinosaur** with **d** or **dr**. He listens for the sounds as the word is stretched out. He writes what he hears. His story is this:

Dinosaurs

Dinosaurs were born in the olden days.

Dinosaurs were big.

Dinosaurs had big teeth.

Dinosaurs had long tails.

Dinosaurs didn't have no food.

```
              Terry

dr

dr y b n oi dz.

d y bg.

d had bg te.

dr hd lg tailz.

dr d h no fd.
```

(Verbally, Terry adds, "That's why we don't have dinosaurs now!")

Stage 3: The Phonetic Stage

The third stage is when vowels appear—though not necessarily the right vowels. The long vowels are correctly represented first, but there is an attempt to represent short vowel sounds also. Regional accents often affect how vowels are represented in this stage.

Paige writes about what she saw at the Nature Science Center. Her writing shows us that her teacher writes predictable charts, and Paige attempts to use this structure in her own writing as she tells us what she saw. (In Paige's writing, **so** represents **saw**. You can hear a short **o** in **saw** if you say it like Paige does.) Her story is this:

I saw a deer.

I saw ducks.

I saw rabbits.

I saw goats.

I saw cows.

I saw a snake.

I saw a wild cat.

```
              paige

i so a der.

i so duks.

i so rabbits.

i so gots.

i so cios.

i so a snak.

i so a wild cat.
```

Stage 4: The Transitional Stage

In this stage, the sounds are represented and the spellings are possible English spellings. When kindergarten students are bright and are allowed to write, they reach this stage quite quickly.

Christopher
I like sienc a lot.
Sienc is fun.
Sienc is neat.
My mom is goeg to git som theings for sienc. I jest got a book abot sienc.
1 books name is 175 sienc etspermets.
The othr books name is hands on sienc.
I love sienc.

Graham
indins got cild a long time a go.
They livd in tpese they fitidid with cow Boys they make thair close out of Bofflows.
They rid horses sumtims the jump off thair horses to ciel snakes to pertek thair horses.
Thair wiepins are nivs.

Christopher

I like science a lot. Science is fun. Science is neat. My mom is going to get some things for science. I just got a book about science. One book's name is 175 Science Experiments. The other book's name is Hands-On Science. I love science.

Graham

Indians got killed a long time ago. They lived in tepees. They fighted (fought) with cowboys. They made their clothes out of buffaloes. They ride horses. Sometimes, they jump off their horses to kill snakes to protect their horses. Their weapons are knives.

Step 5: The Correct Spelling Stage

We have no kindergarten writing samples for Stage 5, because very few kindergarten students can spell all words correctly, unless they limit what they want to say to known spelling words! Kindergartners can be found going through the first four stages as they learn about words and use what they know in daily writing.

How and When Writing Is Multilevel

Writing is a multilevel activity when you let students choose their own topics and take as long as they need to write. Letting students choose their topics guarantees that they are writing about something of which they have knowledge. It also reinforces that what students say and write has worth. As you watch students write, you will learn that some students cannot finish a story in one day. Students at both ends of the spectrum may need more than one day to develop their stories. Some students often have more to say than one writing period allows them to write, while others can write only a few words or lines during that time. Getting several sentences on paper takes some students several days. If you want writing to be a multilevel activity, you must give all students the time that they need to do their best writing.

Phonemic Awareness/Phonics

Rhyming Books

A wonderful winter book to read is *When It Snows* by JoAnne Nelson (Modern Curriculum Press, 1993). This book is written in rhyming questions:

> "Will you dance with your own shadow as it falls across the snow, and wave your arms and fingers so your shadow seems to grow?"

The pictures and questions are fun to talk and think about with any kindergarten class.

Valentine's Day by Miriam Nerlove (Albert Whitman & Company, 1994) is a rhyming book that contains a brief history of Valentine's Day, followed by a girl's account of this celebration at home and at school. Many kindergarten teachers read this book or other similar books to their classes. Do not miss the opportunity to discuss rhyming words as well as the holiday.

Many alphabet books are written in rhyme. *It Begins with an A* by Stephanie Calmenson (Hyperion, 1994) is one example. During the first reading of this book, students usually like to answer the question, "What is it?" for each letter. Read the book a second time and talk about the rhyming words!

Do not forget Dr. Seuss's books! We continue to mention his books because they are rich sources of rhyming words and wonderful examples of word play. *The Cat in the Hat* (Random House, 1957) is a popular book among emerging readers. Read this book to your class. Those students who have heard it before enjoy it just as much as those students who have never heard it. Read it a second time and have students listen for the rhyming pairs of words, including **cat** and **hat** in the title. This book has easy spelling patterns for young students to see and with which they can experiment. There are a lot of words kindergartners know that rhyme with **cat** and **hat**, and it is fun to see how many words they can find.

When reading a rhyming book, let students listen and enjoy it the first time. Then, read it again and round up (find) the rhyming words. If students can easily hear the rhyming pairs, write the words on the board and let them underline the rhyming patterns.

When talking about writing names on Valentine's Day cards, try segmenting the beginning sound (onset) of each name from the remainder of the name (rime).

B–ailey

K–aitlin

P–at

L–afe

M–errill

Making Words

This month, make words with the short vowel patterns **ed**, **et**, **en**, **est**, and **ell**.

Remember the steps for Making Words lessons in kindergarten:

1. Read a book with the selected pattern in the title and/or in the book.

2. Make and read some words with the pattern.

3. Decide what letters to use with the pattern to spell some words. Have students point to each needed letter and have the student with that letter join the other letter students.

Here are the letters, books, and words for the patterns this month:

Pattern: ed
Letters: e d b F f l N s r T w
Book to Read:
Fred and Ted Go Camping by Peter Eastman (Random House, 2005)
Words to Read and Spell: Ted, Fred, bed, fed, led, Ned, red, wed, sled

February

Pattern: et
Letters: e t b g l m n p s w
Book to Read:
Hunky Dory Ate It by Katie Evans (Puffin, 1992)
Read the book. Reread page 12 and talk about the **et** pattern in **pet** and **vet**.
Words to Read and Spell: bet, get, let, met, net, pet, set, wet

Pattern: en
Letters: e n B d h K m p t
Book to Read:
The Little Red Hen, any version
Read the book. Talk about the **en** pattern in **hen** and **then**.
Words to Read and Spell: hen, Ben, den, Ken, men, pen, ten, then

Pattern: est
Letters: e s t t b n p r t v w
Book to Read:
I Ain't Gonna Paint No More by Karen Beaumont (Harcourt Children's Books, 2005)
Read the book. Reread the book to make and spell the words **best**, **nest**, **pest**, **rest**, **test**, **west**, and **vest**.
Words to Read and Spell: best, nest, pest, rest, test, west, vest

Pattern: ell
Letters: e l l b f h s t w y
Book to Read:
The Brand New Kid by Katie Couric (Doubleday, 2000)
Read the book. Reread page 4 and talk about the **ell** pattern in **well** and **swell**.
Words to Read and Spell: bell, fell, sell, well, yell, tell, shell, swell

Tongue Twisters

Tongue twisters help students develop phonemic awareness. As students listen for beginning sounds that are alike in a sentence, their brains become pattern detectors. As they look at the tongue twister, they see the beginning letter in print. Tongue twisters help link phonemic awareness (oral) and phonics (visual).

Students have learned a lot about letters and sounds, so begin placing a new and different tongue twister on the board, on a bulletin board, or in a pocket chart each day during The Opening.

- Point to the words as you read the tongue twister to the class. "Noisy Nora nibbles nutritious nuts."
- Ask the class which words begin alike and what letter is at the beginning of each word.
- Ask students to listen as you read the tongue twister again.

- Ask students if they know any other words that begin with that sound. Almost every student will contribute a word!

Here are some tongue twisters you may want to use with your class:

Aunt Anna always ate apples alone.

Barry Bear has a brown bow and a blue balloon.

Cody's cat carries carrots in a cart.

Damian's dog digs deep down in the dirt.

Ebony the elephant eats every egg.

Felicia and Fred fight for fast food on Friday.

Gus the groundhog gathered goodies from Gail's garden.

Happy Henry happily hugged Hilda and Hank.

Ian Inchworm inches into an igloo.

Jolly Jake jumps for joy in January.

Kami and Katrina Kangaroo keep flying kites.

Little Liann likes to lick a lot of lollipops.

Madeline Mouse munches on marvelous marshmallows.

Noisy Nora nibbles nutritious nuts.

Oliver Octopus eats okra, onions, and oranges.

Pretty Priscilla plants pumpkins in a path.

Ricky Rabbit gives Ruthy Raccoon red roses.

Silly Sally sings seven songs about her senses.

Tom the turkey took ten turtles to town.

The unusual unicorn sat under an umbrella.

Vera has violets, vegetables, a vacuum, and a van.

William the wild wolf went west for the winter.

EXtra! EXtra! Read all about Xx in fox, six, and X-ray.

Yolanda yelled, "Yikes! Get that yak out of my yard!"

A zany zebra zipped a zillion zippers.

Centers

Reading Center

The Reading Center is now filled with many class-made books, as well as a collection of trade books and big books. Students find books they can read and other books they pretend read—but they enjoy the books regardless. The Reading Center is becoming more popular as students find out that a wonderful thing is happening to them—they are becoming **readers**! Students love to share this milestone with family members and friends. Almost every day, a few students will ask to take home books from the Reading Center so that they can share their ability to really read with their families.

Writing Center

The Writing Center is busy this month as students make their own valentines. Many students can now read and write **I love you** inside their cards, and the sentence is on the February word board for students to copy. Some students can add more to their messages as they stretch out the words they want to write. The materials for valentines dominate the Writing Center during the first two weeks of February. After Valentine's Day, students will settle back into copying words for their February Picture Dictionaries from the chart or bulletin board in the Writing Center. Words for the picture dictionary this month can include **love**, **valentines**, **hearts**, **Lincoln**, **Washington**, **Martin Luther King Jr.**, and other special words that students will be discussing this month. Put a picture above each word in the Writing Center so that students who cannot read the words can still use the pictures and their letter-sound knowledge to help them read and write the February words.

Post Office Center

In "Literacy Knowledge in Practice: Contexts of Participation for Young Writers and Readers" (*Reading Research Quarterly*, 32(1), 10–32), Susan Neuman and Kathleen Roskos write about using authentic play settings for students to learn about reading and writing. The centers they suggest help students use reading and writing for real reasons.

A Post Office Center that has paper, stationery, envelopes, pencils, markers, rubber stamps, stamp pads, signs, play money, heart stickers (to be used as stamps), etc., will fit nicely with a February theme. Students can make valentines for their family members this month. Give each student an index card on which you have written her mailing address so that the student can copy the address on the front of an envelope.

Assessing Progress

Continue to help students who did not master all of the tasks on the January assessment. During The Opening, call on students who did not know the days of the week and weather words, giving them a lot of practice so that they can learn these words. Ask students who could not read their classmates' names to help pass back student papers so that they get practice with the names. Continue to read rhyming books and assist students who need extra help with the concept of rhyme. When it is time to talk about familiar words in a new big book, have the whole class listen for how many beats are in the words and clap those beats. Call on students to clap the beats individually, focusing on students who need help with this particular skill.

Use the Kindergarten Assessment Checklist (page 62) when students are reading big books or predictable charts. Ask students to point to the words as they read. Then, ask students if they can show just one word and if they can point to the first and last letters in that word. If students are successful in this task, make notes on their assessment sheets.

Some students may need individual attention for the remainder of the year. Knowing who these students are and the tasks they need to practice will allow you to give them extra instruction as they engage in classroom and center activities with everyone else. Remember, good teachers never give up on their students! Keep nudging them forward.

Assessment of Letter Sounds

To assess students' letter-sound knowledge, say the words listed below and let students write the letters they hear at the beginning and ending of each word on the spaces provided (see page 109). Notice that the vowel is written so that the student does not have to worry about this part of the word—the focus is on beginning and ending consonants only.

Call 3–5 students to a table at the side or back of your classroom or in the Writing Center so that they can do this task at the same time. Make copies of page 109 for each student and say the following:

"I will say a word. Then, I want you to say the word with me. Write the sounds you hear at the beginning and the end of the word on the lines."

1. ham
2. rat
3. fan
4. pad
5. map

Make sure that students are saying each word as they try to write the letters that make the sounds.

February

Here are five more words to say and have students write. Use the reproducible on page 110.

1. red
2. get
3. wet
4. pen
5. bell

Assessment of Letter Sounds

Name_____

Date_____

b d f g h m n p r t w

1. _____ a _____

2. _____ a _____

3. _____ a _____

4. _____ a _____

5. _____ a _____

(See page 107 for directions.)

Assessment of Letter Sounds

Name_____

Date_____

b d f g h l m n p r t w

1. _____e_____

2. _____e_____

3. _____e_____

4. _____e_____

5. _____e_____ _____

(See page 107–108 for directions.)

March

Will March come in like a lion or a lamb? Will it be windy and cold, or will it be warm and springlike? March is a wonderful month to see a wide variety of weather in most areas of the United States and Canada. Many students look forward to having warmer days, playing outside, and watching the landscape turn green. Predicting the weather is almost impossible, but watching and charting the weather can be fun!

The Opening

As you talk about the days of the week, the month, and the date, it is time to call on those late bloomers who now know all of the answers. Listen to their answers when you ask, "What do you notice?" and "How do you know?" You will see how much students have learned since entering kindergarten. It is also time to reflect on what students have learned and what else is needed to prepare them for first grade.

- Can most students count to 100?

- Can most students look at words and cross-check them by beginning sounds?

- Do students know what comes before and after each day of the week and month of the year?

- Can students find the correct weather words?

- Can students place tally marks beside the right words on the weather chart?

- Can students think of words that begin like the words in the tongue twister on the board?

- Do students choose to read and write in centers and when they have free time at home and at school?

- When you write the Morning Message, do students want to help? Are their spelling attempts closer to being correct?

- Can students stretch out words, listen for the sounds, and notice more sound patterns and familiar spelling patterns?

- Does The Opening go quickly and smoothly, even though you have added more to it since the beginning of the year?

When you answer each question, you will see how far the majority of your students have come. The important question is: **Have all students made progress on the journey toward literacy? It is not important that all students are at the same place on this journey.**

> When students come to you with different levels of literacy, you are doing a good job if you accept them where they are and help them move forward in their learning.

Reading Aloud to Students

A favorite book to read to young students is *We're Going on a Bear Hunt* by Michael Rosen (Aladdin, 1993). Especially for students who have been stuck inside for the winter, going on a bear hunt sounds like fun! As students listen to this repetitive story, ask them to imagine going through "splashy, sploshy" water and "squelch, squerch" mud with their families and finding a bear! Students have fun pretending to race home and trying to remember which way to run.

Each student may still be working on an alphabet book from February. An alphabet book to read and enjoy this month is *Potluck* by Anne Shelby (Scholastic, 1993). In the story, everyone is coming for a potluck dinner. "Edmund enters with enchiladas, followed by Fran who furnishes fruit." Guess what Lonnie brings? Lasagna! The alliterative text and illustrations make this book a favorite as students predict who is coming next with what. They have a hint because this is an alphabet book.

Grandma's Helper by Lois Meyer (Pearson, 1993) is a good multicultural book. A little girl helps her grandma shop by translating into English what her grandma says in Spanish. Together, they buy bread, milk, stamps, and oranges. This is another book with repetitive patterns, good illustrations, and a bonus—a focus on Spanish.

Many teachers read Dr. Seuss books during March and celebrate his birthday, especially kindergarten teachers. Some Dr. Seuss books have stories, but some do not. Books like *Hop on Pop* cannot be called fiction or nonfiction; Dr. Seuss was just having fun with words. All of his books are written in rhyme and help students understand how words work.

Some favorite Dr. Seuss books to read this month are:

The Cat in the Hat by Dr. Seuss (Random House, 1957)

The Foot Book by Dr. Seuss (Random House, 1968)

Green Eggs and Ham by Dr. Seuss (Random House, 1960)

Fox in Socks by Dr. Seuss (Random House, 1965)

Hop on Pop by Dr. Seuss (Random House, 1963)

Horton Hatches the Egg by Dr. Seuss (Random House, 1940)

I Can Read with My Eyes Shut! by Dr. Seuss (Random House, 1978)

I Wish That I Had Duck Feet by Dr. Seuss (Random House, 1965)

One Fish Two Fish Red Fish Blue Fish by Dr. Seuss (Random House, 1960)

There's a Wocket in My Pocket! By Dr. Seuss (Random House, 1974)

Ten Apples Up on Top! by Dr. Seuss (Random House, 1961)

Yertle the Turtle and Other Stories by Dr. Seuss (Random House, 1958)

Some other Beginner Books written in Dr. Seuss's style include the following:

Are You My Mother? By P. D. Eastman (Random House, 1960)

Go, Dog, Go! By P. D. Eastman (Random House, 1961)

Put Me in the Zoo by Robert Lopshire (Random House, 1960)

Reading with Students

Shared Reading with Predictable Big Books

Since March is a good month to watch and chart the weather, it is also a good month to read books about weather. One such book is *What Will the Weather Be Like Today?* by Paul Rogers (Scholastic, 1989). This informational book is about the weather and animals in many different places and repeats the question, "What will the weather be like today?" The animals wonder, "Will it be windy? Will it be warm?" just as students ask each day. The book ends with the familiar question, "How is the weather where you are today?"

Before Reading

Take a picture walk and have students predict what this book will be about. Let the pictures on each page help students figure out the words.

During Reading

Read and talk about the book. For the first and second readings of this book, focus on the information in the book and discuss it. The book is full of information, and each page is a story in itself. The book's illustrations will help students talk about different places, different types of weather, and where each type of weather would be found. Does your area have all of these types of weather? This book includes good information for students who have not experienced a wide variety of weather.

Encourage Students to Join in the Reading

The pictures make some parts of *What Will the Weather Be Like Today?* predictable, and the rhyming words help in other parts. Once you have read the book to students several times, they will begin to use the pictures and print to chime in and share the reading. When they see the pictures of kites, sailboats, and hair blowing, they know to say, "Will it be windy?" The next picture shows a summer day, so they will ask, "Will it be warm?"

After Reading

This book does not lend itself to acting out, but it does lend itself to discussion. Play charades in which weather words are pantomimed and guessed by students. Students could show people on a cold day, a windy day, and a rainy day. Students can also talk about their favorite types of weather, draw pictures, and write about them.

Make the Book Available

Remember that students want their favorite books to be read over and over. Then, they pretend that they can read them. Eventually, they will be able to read them! Put this big book and/or the little-book versions of *What Will the Weather Be Like Today?* in the Reading Center for students to enjoy.

Reading by Students

If you have not started Self-Selected Reading, this is a good time to do so. Gather books that students can read or want to read—both fictional and informational books—and put them in a large tub. Give your students five minutes to sit around the tub and read from the books. Some students will be able to read all of the words, especially with easy, predictable, emergent readers or the books read during Shared reading. Remind students before this activity that if they cannot read the words in the books they pick, they can retell the story or read the pictures. Listen to several students and "Ooh!" and "Aah!" at their reading. It is amazing how kindergarten students know whether they are really reading, reading the pictures, or just telling the stories. Five minutes is enough each day for the first week. If everyone can read for five minutes, you might increase it to seven minutes and ten minutes later this month.

Writing for Students

Morning Message

Continue to write a Morning Message for students. At this time of the year, it should be interactive writing—students should help you decide what topic to write about, what to say about the topic, and how to write the words they want to say. Students should also be able to tell you how to begin and end each sentence. You can share the pen with students, but make sure that students you call on can do this task quickly and that their writing is easy to read. Try including a word each day that students will help you write by sounding it out. For example, write "Today we will _____ books at the library." Have students listen for the sounds in **get**. Then, have a student who will be successful write the letters **g**, **e**, and **t** on the three lines. If it is raining outside, write, "Today it is raining. Will we get _____ ?" Have students listen for the three sounds in the word **wet** and write **w**, **e**, and **t** on the lines. Another example is, "I saw a _____ flower." Have students listen for the beginning, middle, and ending sounds in **red** and write **r**, **e**, and **d** on the lines. Modeling this daily will help struggling students learn to stretch out words and sound-spell when they write. Some topics for March Morning Messages include weather, wind and what happens on windy days, the coming of spring, sports, school happenings, themes, and new things that you are teaching.

Writing with Students

Predictable Charts

March is known as the windy month, and a weather unit on wind, reading a book about wind, or talking about wind can lead to writing a predictable chart about things that the wind can blow.

> **The Wind Blew**
>
> The wind blew a balloon. (Adam)
>
> The wind blew a kite. (Quinn)
>
> The wind blew an umbrella. (Michelle)
>
> The wind blew the leaves. (Emily)
>
> The wind blew my hair. (Ty)

Another predictable chart to write in March is about kites. Kites are fun to fly on a windy day in the school yard, a field, or a park. Sometimes, parents will help with this project. Young students like to see the wind lift kites in the air. After watching kites fly and talking about the wind and kites, ask students, "Where would you go if you were a kite? Where would you fly?" Their answers will tell you about the places they would like to visit.

- Ask each student to point to each word in the sentence on the chart as she reads it.

- Give students their sentences and have them cut them apart. (Do not do this for students anymore unless a few students still need support.)

- After they cut the sentences into words, have students place the words on their papers.

- Check to make sure that the word order is correct.

- Have students paste the words on their papers

- Let students illustrate their sentences.

Most students can now draw well, especially kites, and when the book is put together, it is fun to read.

> **A Kite Story**
>
> I would fly to Paris. (Erica)
>
> I would fly to the beach. (Audrey)
>
> I would fly to a hospital. (Adam)
>
> I would fly to Florida. (Riley)
>
> I would fly to see my cousin. (Suzanne)
>
> I would fly to Washington. (William)
>
> I would fly to space. (Rami)
>
> I would fly to New York. (Jasmine)
>
> I would fly to the beach. (Olivia)
>
> I would fly to India. (Nikole)
>
> I would fly to Hawaii. (Michael)
>
> I would fly to my Grandma's. (Kadin)
>
> I would fly to my friends. (Jake)

Here are some examples of students' kite sentences and illustrations:

Writing by Students

Students constantly improve in their writing. As students learn more about letters, sounds, and words, their writing and spelling skills show growth. Since they are discussing kites and the wind, this month many students write stories about kites during writing activities and when they are at the Writing Center. Continue to model stories and think aloud as you write. Model how to use color words that are displayed in the room to help you as you write the story. Stretch out the long words and listen for all of the sounds. Talk as you write:

"If I were a kite, I would be purple and yellow so that everyone could see me. I would fly in the sky. I would fly to my mother's house and see all of my friends."

Students follow your lead, and they choose their favorite colors ("I would be red"). They fly to their favorite places ("I would fly to school"). They tell about the things they see ("I saw a plane"). You may notice that some students do not know about **silent e** yet! Students stretch out their words and write the sounds they hear ("p-e-p-l"). You can read student writing and so can the student who wrote it! As students write, continue to praise their attempts and coach them so that they become even better writers.

Modeling how to write, thinking aloud as you write, and coaching students with their first stories really pays off. It is almost impossible to believe that these are the same students who were drawing pictures and copying words when you asked them to write at the beginning of the school year!

Here are some examples of students' writing at this time:

Ashley

I would fly to New York City.

I saw the world.

I am red and gray.

I saw people.

Nathan

I would fly to Washington, D.C.

My kite is red and blue.

I saw a plane.

Working with Words

Shared Reading followed by Working with Words

Mem Fox is an author known for creating picture books with a strong sense of repetition, like *Hattie and the Fox* (Aladdin, 1988), or rhythm and rhyme, like *Koala Lou* (Voyager, 1988). *Zoo-Looking* by Mem Fox (Mondo, 1996) is a rhyming book that kindergarten students love. This book comes in both little- and big-book sizes. This story is about a girl named Flora. Flora and her father go to the zoo. Flora looks at the animals, and the animals look back! One animal has a snack, another gets a whack, and so on. Before you get very far into this book, students will be listening for the rhymes.

Before Reading

Take a picture walk and talk about the animals Flora meets at the zoo. Use the pictures to help students figure out the names of the animals. Talk about the animals at the zoo. Which are familiar to students (tiger, bear, snake, monkey), and which ones are not familiar (penguin, ostrich, koala)? Reading is a way of introducing students to things that they have never seen.

During Reading

Read and talk about the book. This book is written in rhyme, so students can listen to it, join in, and share the reading. As always, the first time you read the book to students, let them listen to the story and enjoy it. After they have heard it once, students will want to chant along or join in and share the reading. This is especially true if you have the big-book version and students can see the pictures and print easily.

After Reading: Act It Out

Kindergarten students are natural actors and have a good time acting out this story. After choosing two students to be Flora and her father, pick students to be the zoo animals. There are several animals at the zoo, so each student can have a turn if you act out the story two or three times. Each zoo animal can be drawn or copied on a piece of white construction paper. Laminate the pictures, punch two holes at the tops, tie lengths of yarn through the holes, and have students wear the cards so that everyone will know which characters they are.

Reread the story and let students look at each other just as Flora and the zoo animals do during this day at the zoo. How does a snake slither through a crack? How does a bear gobble up a snack? Flora and her father can smile at each other, but her father does not have to pick her up like he does in the story illustration. When students act out stories, they have fun, but it also helps them understand the story. Having Flora look at each animal at the zoo, one by one, also helps students understand the sequence of the story.

Once the book has been read, enjoyed, reread, and acted out, most students can read or pretend read the book. Make the big-book or little-book version that you read to the class available in the Reading Center so that students can enjoy this book again and again.

Rounding Up the Rhymes

Read the story another day. Students do not get tired of listening to the story because of its rhythm and rhyme. Ask students to listen for the rhyming words. If you have been reading rhyming books and talking about rhyming words, this should be an easy task for them!

- Read the story again and ask students to help you round up the words that rhyme with **back**. Students find **black**, **crack**, **smack**, **whack**, **snack**, and **yak**.

- Write the rhyming words on the board or on a chart as you and students find them in the story.

- Then, ask, "What do you notice?" See if students notice the same spelling pattern in all of the words except **yak**. Explain that most of the time, but not always, words that rhyme with **back** are spelled with the **a–c–k** spelling pattern.

Making Words

Work on phonemic awareness with students by segmenting and blending letters and sounds and doing Making Words activities. Using the laminated cards you made or the letter vests you purchased (see page 80), students can become letters. Choose three students: one for the **a** card, one for the **c** card, and one for the **k** card. These students become the **ack** rhyme or spelling pattern. Choose other students to be the letters **b**, **c**, **j**, **m**, **n**, **p**, **r**, **s**, **t**, and **z**. Let students whose cards spell **back** stand in front of the class. Say the letters **b**, **a**, **c**, and **k** and the word **back** aloud. Take away the **b** by having that student sit down. Say aloud what is left—**ack**. Have each of the other students holding a letter stand with **ack**. Let

students notice that it is important that they stand in front of **a–c–k**. See which students can read the new words as students who are holding letter cards join **a–c–k** to become new words, such as **Jack**, **pack**, **rack**, **sack**, **tack**, **Zack**, **crack**, **smack**, or **snack**.

This manipulation of letters and sounds to make new words is an important part of learning how to read. Making Words is a wonderful way to introduce the concepts of onset and rime. Young students understand things they can see, and being the letters and making words is an excellent way for students to see how beginning sounds and spelling patterns come together to make many different words. It also helps students to see how changing one letter can change the word!

Making Words Lessons

This month, do Making Words lessons with the short vowel patterns **it**, **in**, **ip**, **ill**, **ick**, **op**, **ot**, and **og**.

Remember the steps for Making Words lessons in kindergarten:

1. Read a book with the selected pattern in the title and/or in the book.

2. Make and read some words with the pattern.

3. Decide what letters to use with the pattern to spell some words. Have students point to each needed letter and have the student with that letter join the other letter students.

Here are the letters, books, and words for each pattern this month:

Pattern: it
Letters: i t b f h k l p s
Book to Read:
The Cat in the Hat by Dr. Seuss (Random House, 1957)
Read the book. Reread page 3. Talk about the **it** pattern in **sit**, **it**, and **bit**.
Words to Make and Spell: bit, fit, hit, kit, lit, pit, sit, skit

Pattern: in
Letters: i n b c f h k p s t w
Book to Read:
The Three Little Pigs, any version
Read the book. Reread the pages on which the wolf says, "Not by the hair of my chinny **chin chin**."
Words to Make and Spell: bin, chin, fin, kin, pin, sin, tin, win, skin

Pattern: ip
Letters: i p d h k l r s t z
Book to Read:
Miss Bindergarten Stays Home from Kindergarten by Joseph Slate (Puffin, 2000)
Read the book. Reread pages 19–20. Talk about the **ip** pattern in **sip** and **dip**.
Words to Make and Spell: dip, hip, lip, rip, sip, tip, zip, skip

Pattern: ill
Letters: i l l B f h J k p w
Book to Read:
Each Peach Pear Plum by Janet Ahlberg and Allan Ahlberg (Puffin, 1978)
Read the book. Reread page 14: "Bo-Peep up the **hill**. I spy Jack and **Jill**." Talk about the **ill** pattern.
Words to Make and Spell: Jill, Bill, fill, hill, kill, pill, will

Pattern: ick
Letters: i c k D l N p R r s t
Book to Read:
Miss Bindergarten Stays Home from Kindergarten by Joseph Slate (Puffin, 2000)
Read the book. Reread pages 21–22. Talk about the **ick** pattern in **trick** and **sick**.
Words to Make and Spell: Dick, lick, Nick, pick, Rick, sick, tick, stick, trick

March ··

Pattern: op

Letters: o p b d h m p s r t

Book to Read:

Hop on Pop by Dr. Seuss (Random House, 1963)

Read the book. Reread pages 40–41. Talk about the **op** pattern in **hop**, **pop**, and **stop**.

Words to Make and Spell: bop, hop, pop, mop, top, stop, drop

Pattern: ot

Letters: o t c d g h l p s

Book to Read:

The Cat in the Hat by Dr. Seuss (Random House, 1957)

Read the book. Reread page 27. Talk about the **ot** pattern in **lot** and **pot**.

Words to Make and Spell: cot, dot, got, hot, lot, pot, slot

Pattern: og

Letters: o g d f h j l r

Book to Read:

"To Market, To Market" in any collection of nursery rhymes

Read the rhyme. Talk about the **og** pattern in **hog** and **jog**.

Words to Make and Spell: dog, fog, hog, log, jog, frog

Centers

Reading Center

The Reading Center is filled with many alphabet books, including class-made books. Students are spending time reading their favorite books, usually ones they can actually read. Pretend reading still happens, but students know when they pick a book whether they will be able to really read it or if they will enjoy the pictures and pretend read it. It is amazing that kindergarten students can accurately assess their reading abilities with each book they pick up.

Read several new books and add them to the Reading Center. Add weather books, books about wind, and leprechaun stories. Students love to hear leprechaun stories around St. Patrick's Day. Sometimes, you may want to focus on the Easter holiday during March. That would mean reading more books about bunnies and eggs.

Writing Center

As kindergartners learn more about writing and get better at doing it, the Writing Center becomes more popular than ever. The computer is a favorite piece of equipment. Students have discovered that it makes writing their stories easier, and handwriting is no longer a problem. Along with copying the March Picture Dictionary chart or bulletin board, students can write letters and notes to people they know. If you have a commercial picture dictionary, put it in the Writing Center. Some students may want to check the spellings of words.

Travel Agency or Doctor's Office Center

In February, you added a Post Office Center. March is a good month to add a Travel Agency Center for all of those places that students want their kites to fly to. What would you put in this center? Posters, a calendar, a computer, paper, pencils, markers, travel brochures, etc., are all good choices.

Another possibility is a Doctor's Office or Health Clinic Center. This center could have an appointment book, pencils, markers, a calendar, a notepad, play money, insurance forms, file folders, a clipboard, an eye chart, a doctor's bag, a stethoscope, etc. Students could pretend to be patients, doctors, nurses, or secretaries. Here, students can read, pretend read, write, or pretend write for real reasons!

Assessing Progress

March marks the end of the third quarter in many schools. It is time to look at the progress students have made. Assessment is not something that you do only once every quarter, but it is something that you do daily as you watch students and take note of each student's progress. Assessing this progress involves looking at the names and words that students know and looking at their phonemic awareness and how it is developing. Phonemic awareness, the ability to manipulate words, includes knowing that the sentence "I had a bad day at school today" has more words than the sentence "I got mad."

Phonemic awareness also includes being able to clap syllables in words and knowing that the word **automobile** takes more claps than the word **car**. Perhaps the most critical phonemic awareness skill to assess toward the end of kindergarten is the ability to come up with a word that rhymes with another word. Students who have phonemic awareness can tell you that **bike** rhymes with **Mike** and that **book** does not rhyme with **Mike**. Assess this phonemic awareness skill by observing each student's ability to do rhyming-word tasks as you are doing activities with the whole class. As you begin April activities, most students will have the desired level of phonemic awareness, and you will need to know which students need continued nudges toward developing this.

Assessing Letter Sounds

Many students have learned some letter names and sounds. Some students can recognize all 26 letters and know the sounds that these letters make in words. Other students usually recognize all 26 letters in both uppercase and lowercase forms and have learned sounds for the most common letters. Usually, the letter names and sounds that students know are based on the words that they can read and write. Students typically know the letters in their names and the names of their friends.

Last month's assessment focused on letter-sound knowledge. The assessment this month will also focus on letter-sound knowledge. To assess letter-sound knowledge again, call 3–5 students to a table at the side or the back of the classroom so that they can complete the task at the same time. Make copies of page 125 for each student. Notice that the vowel is written so that the student needs to focus on only the beginning and ending consonants.

"I will say a word. Then, I want you to say the word with me. Write the sounds at the beginning and the end of the word on the lines."

1. pin
2. rip
3. bit
4. fin
5. hill

Here are five more words to say with students and have them write. Use the reproducible on page 126.

1. top
2. dog
3. hot
4. log
5. hop

Assessment of Letter Sounds

Name_____

Date_____

b d f g h j l m n p r s t w

1. _____ i _____

2. _____ i _____

3. _____ i _____

4. _____ i _____

5. _____ i _____ _____

(See page 124 for directions.)

Assessment of Letter Sounds

Name_____

Date_____

b   d   f   g   h   j   l   m   n   p   r   s   t   w

1. _____ o _____

2. _____ o _____

3. _____ o _____

4. _____ o _____

5. _____ o _____

(See page 124 for directions.)

April

Spring is finally here! Warmer days are pleasant signs of what is to come. Many students have a spring break to anticipate. There is a lot to learn at school and within the community. Flowers and trees bloom. Planting season begins in many areas. Baby animals are being born, and signs of new life are everywhere. Help students see the changes and understand what is happening in their world and why.

The Opening

"Who is at school today? Is anyone absent? What day of the week is it? What is the month? Date? Year? How many days have we been in school? Can anyone count them? Let's make a mark for each day." Add a straw to the jar. The straws have been grouped into bundles of ten and a hundreds bundle, and students count with you. Count hundreds first, tens next, and then ones to find out how many days students have been in school. The calendar for April is on the bulletin board where students can see it as you talk about the now-familiar days of the week and the date and chart the weather each day.

Once again, draw students' attention to the beginnings of words on the calendar and the bulletin board by asking familiar questions, such as the following:

"Can you find the word **Tuesday** on the calendar?"

"How do you know that this says **Tuesday**?"

"What do you notice about the word **Tuesday**?"

"How do you know it is not **Thursday**? **Thursday** begins with **T** also."

Students will probably tell you that **Thursday** has **th** at the beginning. Students who have learned letter names and the sounds they represent at the beginnings of words are now ready to listen for more than one sound at the beginnings of words.

Morning Message

When you write the Morning Message, you may notice that students want to do the thinking and spelling. Many students have things that they want to say each morning. When asked to spell the high-frequency words, they can! Practice and repetition have made these words familiar for some kindergartners.

When students are doing most of the work, you know that there is a lot of learning going on! **Let students spell the longer, harder words as you stretch them out.** Write exactly what they tell you. You will notice that some students can spell many words correctly by this time. **When their spelling is close, do not change it.** You want to show students what people do when they do not know how to spell a word. They do not change **enormous** to **big** because they cannot spell

enormous. Instead, they write **enormous** and spell it as best they can. **Coaching students to invent the spellings of words that they do not know pays off. Invented spelling helps these students think about how words sound and how they are spelled.** Some words will still trick them, but some words still trick adults!

Once Easter has come and gone, spring is the big topic during April. Some students will share their plans for spring break. When students talk about their experiences for the Morning Message, they use big voices and speak in complete sentences as they have been told to do all year. For some students, the few small words they uttered at the beginning of kindergarten have become long, complete sentences that give other students new information. **For many students, language has improved by talking and listening during The Opening each morning.**

Reading Aloud to Students

There are many books about spring, animal babies, and spring holidays to read to students. What you read depends on the customs and culture in your community and the themes you plan to teach this month. Books about planting a garden and baby animals are popular with kindergarten teachers and students.

Books to Read in April

All About Seeds by Susan Kuchalla (Troll Communications, 1982)

Babies on the Go by Linda Ashman (Harcourt Children's Books, 2003)

Bad Kitty (Three alphabet books in one!) by Nick Bruel (Roaring Brook Press, 2005)

The Carrot Seed by Ruth Krauss (HarperCollins, 1945)

Does a Kangaroo Have a Mother, Too? by Eric Carle (HarperTrophy, 2000)

I Like the Rain by Claude Belanger (Shortland, 1988)

It Looked Like Spilt Milk by Charles G. Shaw (HarperTrophy, 1988)

It's Spring by Else Holmelund Minarik (Greenwillow, 1989)

The Lamb and the Butterfly by Arnold Sundgaard (Scholastic, 1988)

Over in the Meadow by Ezra Jack Keats (Puffin, 1999)

Owen's Marshmallow Chick by Kevin Henkes (HarperCollins, 2002)

The Secret Birthday Message by Eric Carle (HarperTrophy, 1971)

Two Eyes, a Nose, and a Mouth by Roberta Grobel Intrater (Scholastic, 2000)

Vegetable Garden by Douglas Florian (Voyager, 1991)

The Very Hungry Caterpillar by Eric Carle (Penguin, 1987)

Reading with Students

Shared Reading with Predictable Big Books

April is known as the rainy month. *I Like the Rain* by Claude Belanger (Shortland, 1988) is a read-together, sing-together book about weather. *Rain* by Robert Kalan (HarperTrophy, 1991) is a book about rain and is available as a big book. The big-book format's predictable pictures and text are wonderful for shared reading. You can review color words while reading this book.

Before Reading

Take a picture walk through *Rain*. Notice what is happening in each picture, talk about each picture, and point out how the word **rain** is spelled. Ask students, "What is that word? What letters are in the word?"

During Reading

Read and talk about the book. The first and second readings should focus on the meaning and enjoyment of the book. When you read the book to your class, pause occasionally to talk about the pictures and the print (blue sky, yellow sun, white clouds, gray clouds, gray sky, etc.). Reread the story and help students notice the repeating pattern: Rain on _____ (color word, object). Do they notice that the rain in the picture is really the word **rain**? How does the story end? Have students ever seen a rainbow after it rains? Many kindergarten students have never seen a rainbow but are fascinated by them. After reading this story, students will begin to look in the sky after it rains to find a rainbow!

Encourage Students to Join in the Reading

After you have read the book to students, let them echo-read the pages by repeating the words after you. Another way to reread the book is to have students join in the reading. Assign a color to each student and let the student read the page(s) with his color word on it. All students love to join in and share the reading once the rain begins ("Rain on the green grass" and "Rain on the black road"), and students love to say **rainbow** at the end.

After Reading: Act It Out

Lead the class in a discussion about the book. Talk about the sequence, colors, etc.

Students can act out the story! Write color words on cards and tie yarn of the same color to the top of each card. Students can wear the cards like necklaces.

Blue says, "Blue sky."

Yellow says, "Yellow sun."

White says, "White clouds."

Gray says, "Gray clouds."

Then, when the rain comes, students who are the other colors say their parts:

> Green says, "Rain on the green grass."

> Black says, "Rain on the black roads."

At the end of the book, all students stand and say, "Rainbow!"

Make the Book Available

When students hear and enjoy a book that you have read to the whole class, they like to pick it up later by themselves and enjoy it again. Because of the pictures and color words, *Rain* is an easy story for some students to read by themselves. The pictures make pretend reading easier for those who are still at that stage. Sometimes, you may see several students sit together with a book and help each other read it. Listen to their prompts to each other—you will hear yourself! Young students learn to do what they see. If students see you circulating and helping students reread books, they will do the same.

Writing with Students

Predictable Charts

Predictable charts lead to more class books, and both spring and rain are good topics for predictable charts. After reading the book *Where Does the Butterfly Go When It Rains?* by May Garelick (Mondo, 1961), students will be ready to tell you where they think the butterfly will go. Write the title of the book at the top of a piece of chart paper. Then, write students' responses to the question.

Touch Reading

On the following day, have each student touch read her own sentence, touching each word as she reads it. This is a way to see if each child is tracking print and developing voice-to-print match.

Sentence Builders

The next day, write several sentences from the chart on sentence strips and cut them into words. Take the words from one sentence and give them to students. Let students find their places as they build the sentence. Ask the first student, "Why are you standing at the beginning of the sentence?" See if the student says that the capital letter at the beginning of his word

---

Where Does the Butterfly Go When it Rains?

. . . in a tree. (Ryan)

. . . in a hole. (Adam)

. . . in a bush. (William)

. . . under a branch. (Olivia)

. . . to his home. (Michelle)

. . . in the grass. (Mitchell)

. . . under a basket. (Suzanne)

. . . in a tree. (Refugio)

. . . under a box. (Paul)

. . . in a flower. (Jasmine)

. . .under a chair. (Emily)

. . . some place sunny. (Richard)

. . . under a porch. (Rayshawn)

. . . in a cocoon. (Nikki)

. . . in a window. (Julie)

. . . to live with other bugs. (Jimmy)

. . . under some place. (Tiara)

. . . in a house. (Erica)

. . . under a leaf. (Mike)

. . . in a tent. (Jacob)

---

helped determine where he would stand. See if the last student will tell you that the period at the end of her word showed her where to stand. After students build each sentence by standing in order with their words in front of them, read the words aloud so that the rest of the class can check to see if the sentence is correct.

Making a Class Book

After several sentences have been built, it is time for each student to cut apart the words in his sentence and put the words in order. Check to see that the words are in the right order in each child's sentence before students paste the words on paper. Some students may still need help with this, but others will find it simple. Finally, ask students to illustrate their sentences. Students should draw big butterflies and the places they think the butterflies will go if it rains. Students can draw rain in their pictures. After students illustrate their sentences, help them put the class book in order by lining up with their pages, using the predictable chart as a guide. Add front and back covers to the pages using colorful construction paper. Write the title of the class book on the front cover with a thick black marker. Draw a big butterfly, or cut one from a magazine and paste it to the front cover. Now, you have another book that most students can read.

Other Ideas for Predictable Charts

Another book that lends itself to making a predictable chart is *What's In My Pocket?* by Rozanne Lanczak Williams (Creative Teaching Press, 1994). After reading and enjoying the book, make a predictable chart with students and let students answer the question, "What's in my pocket?" All of their responses should begin with "In my pocket is . . . ."

Writing by Students

Students' writing continues to improve as they learn more about letters and sounds. The words that students are writing and spelling show this growth. Since April is the time to discuss spring and rain, students often choose to write stories about those subjects. Continue to model stories and think aloud as you write. Stretch out long words and have students listen for the sounds. Talk as you write:

"It is spring. (**Spring** is on the bulletin board, and I can copy it from there.)"

"The weather is warm and sunny. (**Warm** and **sunny** are words that we use many mornings. I can find weather words listed near where we do The Opening each morning.)"

"The grass is green. (**Green** is a color word, and I see it written there.)"

"The trees are green. (I can find **green** in the sentence above.)"

"We can play outside and have fun!"

April

Students will follow your lead. When it rains, many students will write about the rain. Students tell about the things they see. They stretch out their words and write the sounds they hear in words. As students write, continue to coach them and praise their attempts.

In kindergarten, celebrate what each student can do, especially what he can do when he writes. Do not ask kindergartners to spell words correctly—they cannot! If you ask them to use only words they know how to spell, you will not see the same growth in their writing and spelling skills. Share each child's growth with her parents by showing them writing samples collected throughout the year. Most parents are amazed at their child's writing! Some parents may need to be reassured that students will learn to edit stories and begin to work on the correct spellings of high-frequency words in first grade.

Here are some examples of student writing at this time of year:

Africa	Africa
Jaleel	Jaleel
My mom livd in Afroco.	My mom lived in Africa.
Afroco is a fon plas.	Africa is a fun place.
Wot kins of masks r thair?	What kinds of masks are there?
Thair is liens in Afroco.	There are lions in Africa.
Thair or mnnecis in Afroco.	There are monkeys in Africa.
Ejip is in Afroco.	Egypt is in Africa.
Did you no that thair r sites in Afroco?	Did you know that there are sights in Africa?
I wish I cod go to Afroco.	I wish I could go to Africa.

My Pet	My Pet
Sam	Sam
I have a pet.	I have a pet.
It is a dog.	It is a dog.
I like hr a lot.	I like her a lot.
I lay waf my dog.	I lay with my dog.
I play waf my dog.	I play with my dog.
I lay waf my dog at nit.	I lay with my dog at night.
I red hr dog books.	I read her dog books.
I tac hr to the vat.	I take her to the vet.
I love my dog.	I love my dog.

If your school has a computer lab, take advantage of it! Some kindergarten classes go to the computer lab each day for their writing time. Let students write at either the computers or their desks. Everyone writes, and at the end of this writing time, several students share what they wrote in an Author's Chair format. **Sharing stories gives young authors new writing ideas because they hear what classmates wrote about—topics familiar to them. It also gives students another audience for their work.**

Working with Words

Making Words

This month, do Making Words lessons with the short vowel patterns **ug**, **ub**, **un**, **ut**, **ump, and**, **end,** and **ing**.

Remember the steps for Making Words lessons in kindergarten:

1. Read a book with the selected pattern in the title and/or in the book.

2. Make and read some words with the pattern.

3. Decide what letters to use with the pattern to spell some words. Have students point to each needed letter and have the student with that letter join the other letter students.

Here are the letters, books, and words for each pattern this month:

Making Words Lessons

Pattern: ug

Letters: u g b d h j m p r t

Book to Read:

There's a Bug in My Mug by Kent Salisbury (Learning Horizons, 1997)

Read the book. Talk about the **ug** pattern in the title and the first pair of rhymes: "Who's in my **mug**? A big green **bug**!"

Words to Make and Spell: bug, dug, hug, jug, mug, pug, rug, tug

Pattern: ub

Letters: u b c d h l p r s t

Book to Read:

The rhyme "Rub a Dub, Dub, Three Men in a Tub" found in any Nursery Rhymes collection.

Read the rhyme. Talk about the **ub** pattern in **rub**, **dub**, and **tub**.

Words to Make and Spell: cub, hub, pub, tub, rub, sub, dub, club, stub

April

Pattern: un

Letters: u n b f g r s

Book to Read:

One Fish Two Fish Red Fish Blue Fish by Dr. Seuss (Random House, 1960)

Read the book. Reread page 10. Talk about the **un** pattern in **run**, **fun**, and **sun**.

Words to Make and Spell: bun, fun, gun, sun, run

Pattern: ut

Letters: u t b c h n r s

Book to Read:

I Can Read with My Eyes Shut! by Dr. Seuss (Random House, 1978)

Read the book. Reread page 28. Talk about the **ut** pattern in **Hut–Zut** and **shut**.

Words to Make and Spell: but, cut, hut, nut, rut, shut

Pattern: ump

Letters: u m p b d h j l p s t

Book to Read:

One Fish Two Fish Red Fish Blue Fish by Dr. Seuss (Random House, 1960)

Read the book. Reread pages 18–19. Talk about the **ump** pattern in **bump**, **wump**, **hump**, **gump**, and **jump**.

Words to Make and Spell: bump, dump, hump, jump, lump, pump, stump

Pattern: and

Letters: a n d b h l s t

Book to Read:

Miss Spider's Tea Party by David Kirk (Scholastic, 1994)

Read the book. Reread page 4. Talk about the **and** pattern in **demand** and **hand**.

Words to Make and Spell: band, hand, land, sand, stand

Pattern: end

Letters: e n d b l m p s

Books to Read:

My Friends by Taro Gomi (Chronicle, 1990)

Read the book. Reread several pages. Talk about the **end** pattern in **friend** and **end**.

Words to Make and Spell: bend, lend, mend, send, spend, blend

Pattern: ing
Letters: i n g b k r s t w
Book to Read:
One Fish Two Fish Red Fish Blue Fish by Dr. Seuss (Random House, 1960)
Read the book. Reread page 40. Talk about the **ing** pattern in **Ying**, **sing**, and **anything**.
Words to Make and Spell: bing, king, ring, sing, wing, bring, sting

Tongue Twisters

Teachers often add tongue twisters at the end of kindergarten. Write the following sentence on the board: **Charlie Chipmunk chooses to chomp cherry cheesecake.** Ask students what they notice about this tongue twister.

A student may answer that many of the words begin with **ch**, two letters that make one sound! Ask students to say the **ch** words with you and listen for the **ch** sound at the beginnings of the words. Are the beginning sounds the same for those words with **ch** at the beginning? Yes!

This month, add digraph tongue twisters to your list, such as these:

Thirsty Thelma is thankful for her Thermos®.

Thirsty Thelma thinks that's great.

Shawn showed Shirley his shiny new shoes.

Whitney the white whale whistles and whirls.

Environmental Print: Cereals

Students must practice to improve their reading and writing skills and word knowledge. Some students see their families reading books and magazines and writing on a daily basis. Others do not have books and magazines at home. At home, students should practice some of the things they do in school.

One way to practice is to use environmental print. **Most students know their favorite cereals, drinks, and fast-food restaurants. Many children and adults who cannot read can recognize the logos of products they see and use.** If you want students to practice letter names at home, teach them how to do this by using the cereal boxes found in their homes. Bring in several boxes from different types of popular cereals or have students bring in empty boxes. Talk about cereal and ask how many students eat it for breakfast each day. Graph the class's favorite cereals to find out which brands/types are the most popular.

Start with the class's favorite cereal. Hold up the box and have students look at it. Talk about the colors and the pictures on the box. Have students count the letters in the cereal's name with you. For example, if the class's favorite cereal is **Cheerios®**, start with it. Count, "1–2–3–4–5–6–7–8. There are eight letters in **Cheerios®**." Have students say the letter names with you ("C–h–e–e–r–i–o–s").

Next, pass out laminated letter cards. The letters should be identical to the letters on the box. Ask, "Who has the **C**? **h**? **e**? **e**? **r**? **i**? **o**? **s**?" Have students stand in order to spell **Cheerios®**. As you point to each student with a letter card, have the student say her letter. Then, collect the letters and have students return to their seats.

Hold up the box again. Ask, "What do you notice about the box?" You may hear responses like the following:

"**Cheerios®** begins with a capital **C**."

"The box is yellow."

"It begins with a **ch** sound, like **Charles**."

"There is an **o** in **Cheerios**."

"It ends with **s**."

After discussing the box, the cereal name, and the letters, place the laminated letters in the pocket chart to form the word. Let students write **Cheerios®** with black crayons or markers and have them draw pictures of the box.

Once you have done the activity with several cereals, students will have a way to practice letter names at home. Students enjoy showing what they have learned in school, and environmental print gives them that opportunity each day even if they do not come from homes with books and magazines.

Note: The brand name used in the previous exercise is not owned by or affiliated with Carson-Dellosa Publishing Company, Inc., in any way and is used for illustrative purposes only. General Mills, Inc., is the exclusive license of the registered trademark Cheerios®.

Centers

Reading Center

Centers are tied closely to the themes students are studying at this time of year. Students are studying spring and rain this month, so books and stories about plants and growing vegetables in spring are found in the Reading Center. You can also begin placing signs in each center telling students what to do. When some students can read the signs, they will help others who cannot.

Writing Center

Put materials in the Writing Center for students to make signs for their home gardens. The April Picture Dictionary chart or bulletin board has words for the parts of a plant. Students enjoy using the computer in the Writing Center because they can write so much more when they use it. Make sure that all students have a chance to write on the computer.

Grocery Store Center

In April, add a Grocery Store Center and expand your study of environmental print. Use cereal boxes and other familiar grocery items to help students learn about letters. Place empty cans and food boxes in the center. (Make sure that there are no sharp edges on the cans and boxes!) You may also include a cash register, play money, a basket or play grocery cart, notepads for grocery lists, and bags. Students can pretend to be cashiers, baggers, or customers who can buy whatever they need or want!

April

Assessing Progress

Assessing Letter Sounds

Last month's assessment focused on letter-sound knowledge. To assess this knowledge again, do a similar task. Call 3–5 students to a table at the side or the back of the classroom so that they can complete the task at the same time. Make copies of page 139 for each student. Notice that the vowel is written so that each child can focus on only the beginning and ending consonants.

"I will say a word. Then, I want you to say the word with me. Write the sounds you hear at the beginning and the end of the word on the lines."

1. hug

2. rub

3. sun

4. nut

5. jump

In the last months of kindergarten, most students will have the desired level of phonemic awareness. You have been working on letter names and letter sounds, and most students have learned these concepts. You know which students need extra help to continue to develop this skill. Many students also know some words that pop up in their reading and writing. Some teachers call these words high-frequency words or popcorn words and will assess these words this month.

Assessment of Letter Sounds

Name_____

Date_____

b d f g h j l m n p r s t w

1. _____ u _____

2. _____ u _____

3. _____ u _____

4. _____ u _____

5. _____ u _____ _____

(See page 138 for directions.)

May/June

The end of the school year is in sight! Many teachers wonder whether they will finish everything they wanted to accomplish this year. For most, the answer is yes, but they still worry. Why? Teachers never see the jobs of teaching and learning as fully accomplished! You see a portion of the task completed each year, but no child has accomplished everything of which she is capable. Learning takes a lifetime, not just one year in kindergarten!

Some students are sad that the school year is coming to an end—they will miss the teacher whom they have come to respect and love. Other students will miss their new friends whom they will not see again until the next school year. Some also worry about what first grade will be like and who their first-grade teacher will be!

If you have been doing multilevel activities as described, most of your students are ready for first grade. The students about whom you were most worried have come the farthest. As a kindergarten teacher, you cannot make up five years of literacy learning in one year, but you can narrow the gap and get students on the road to learning by providing them with the same experiences that students who come from more literate homes have had. That is what the activities in the previous chapters were meant to do.

If you have been doing multilevel activities and accepting the approximations that students make, all students should have moved forward. If not, look carefully at their attempts and your actions. Are you providing the support that each student needs in his literacy learning? Are your expectations within students' limits? Are you celebrating their successes?

The Opening

The Opening continues to the last day of school. This is a time to celebrate how well students do with The Opening tasks. The familiar questions were not familiar at one time. Students now know the days of the week, the date, and weather words. They can read many of these words. Students know with what letter a word begins and several other words that begin with the same letter. They know about rhyming words and how changing a beginning sound can change a word. They have phonemic awareness and are ready for phonics instruction in first grade. They are also ready for many of the reading and writing tasks they will do in the coming year. These students have learned to think about words and how words work, and this will continue in first grade. Tongue Twisters, the Morning Message, and new books can be a part of The Opening as students listen for and talk about letters and letter sounds.

As the end of the school year gets closer, discuss end-of-the-year events—field trips, class picnics, field day, awards day, etc. Also, discuss a few new activities that will prepare students for the transition to first grade. These activities are discussed so that students will be aware of why the routine changes and what will be expected of them as they enter first grade. It will also help make the beginning of the year easier for them.

Reading Aloud to Students

There are a lot of books about flowers, bugs, and summer activities to read to students. With the year coming to an end, it is a good time to also read class favorites. Ask students about their favorite stories, books, and authors. Graph their favorites and see which books they remember and enjoyed.

Bright Eyes, Brown Skin by Cheryl Willis Hudson and Bernette G. Ford (Just Us Books, 1990) This book is about four new school friends. Students in the story love to do some of the same things that your students have done at school this year—draw, dance, clap, read, dress up, and play make-believe. Discuss the illustrations in the book and listen for the rhymes.

Chickens on the Go! by Judith A. McEwen (www.chickensonthego.com, 2006) This is a cute book to read at the end of the year. It is about how chickens are different around the world (CanadiHENS, AfricHENS, PolynesHENS, BritHENS, JapHENese, RusHENS, MexicHENS, and AmericHENS) and yet whatever you call them, they are all chickens! Even kindergarten students will understand this message of tolerance and acceptance.

Pebble Books Series by Cheryl Coughlan (Capstone Press) This series is about insects. Reading these books to students gives them information about the bugs they may meet this summer. Books in this series include *Ants* (1999), *Beetles* (1999), *Bumble Bees* (2000), *Crickets* (1999), *Dragonflies* (2000), *Flies* (1999), *Grasshoppers* (1999), *Ladybugs* (2000), and *Mosquitoes* (1999).

Popular Books for May/June

Airplanes by Lola M. Schaefer (Bridgestone, 1999) Other books in this series include:

   Bicycles (Heinemann, 2003)

   Cable Cars (Bridgestone, 1999)

   Ferries (Bridgestone, 2000)

   Trains (Heinemann, 2003)

Animal Mothers by Atsushi Komori (Houghton Mifflin, 1996)

Berenstain Bears Go to Camp by Stan Berenstain and Jan Berenstain (Random House, 1982)

Bugs, Bugs, Bugs! by Jennifer Dussling (DK Children, 1999)

May/June ....

City Mouse–Country Mouse and Two More Mouse Tales from Aesop by Aesop (Scholastic, 1987)

Dibble and Dabble by Dave Saunders and Julie Saunders (Simon and Schuster Children's Publishing, 1990)

Emma Kate by Patricia Polacco (Scholastic, 2005)

The Gunnywolf by A. Delaney (HarperCollins, 1992)

Have You Seen My Cat? by Eric Carle (Aladdin, 1988)

I Know an Old Lady Who Swallowed a Fly: A Traditional Rhyme by Slug Signorino (Diane Publishing Company, 1993)

The Incredible Book Eating Boy by Oliver Jeffers (Philomel Books, 2007)

Ladybugs and Other Insects by Gallimard Jeunesse (Scholastic, 2007)

On the Go by Ann Morris (HarperTrophy, 1994)

The Story of Ferdinand by Munro Leaf (Scholastic, 1964)

Summer Stinks by Marty Kelley (Zino Press Children's Books, 2001)

The Very Busy Spider by Eric Carle (Penguin, 1984)

Wonders of Plants and Flowers by Laura Damon (Troll Associates, 1990)

Reading with Students

Shared Reading with Predictable Big Books

May and June are usually warm and sunny months with days that give hints of the summer. In May, celebrate Mother's Day, and in June, celebrate Father's Day—if you go to school that late in June! A good book for shared reading around Mother's Day is *Animal Mothers* by Atsushi Komori (Houghton Mifflin, 1996). *On the Go* by Ann Morris (HarperTrophy, 1994) is a story of a trip around the world told in photographs. This nonfiction book has bicycles, horses, buses, trains, boats, cars, planes, and rockets—everything students know or need to know about the ways people go places.

Another book that is fun to read and meets all of the criteria for Shared reading is *Me Too!* by Mercer Mayer (Random House, 1996). This is the story of a brother who tells many things that he does and of his little sister who always yells, "Me too!" What does the brother do? He helps his little sister do the things that he does.

Before Reading

Take a picture walk through *Me Too!*. Look at the pictures and talk about them. Ask students to predict what happens in the story by looking at what happens in the pictures.

During Reading

The first reading of *Me Too!* should focus on the meaning and enjoyment of the book. Talk about the cover, the title of the book, and the author. Can students read the title? Choose someone to read the title aloud as you point to the words.

Read the book again, pausing occasionally to talk about the pictures and the print. Encourage students to tell what other things the little sister might want to do. Has anyone in your class had this experience with a sister or brother? Let each student tell the class about it.

Encourage Students to Join in the Reading

Reread the story a third time and encourage students to join in with the words they know. All students should join in when the sister says, "Me too!" As you read the book, pause and allow students to comment on the illustrations and predict what will happen next. Then, turn the page and find out if students are correct. Sometimes, students will predict correctly. Sometimes, students are wrong but could have been right. Talk about their predictions: why some are good predictions and why some do not make sense for this story.

After Reading

Talk about the things that brothers and sisters do together. What time of year is it when each event in the story takes place, and how do students know? Which things in the book can students do? Which things will students do this summer? Has anyone in the class ever yelled, "Me too!" to a brother or sister? Has a brother, sister, or friend ever yelled this to anyone in your class?

Act It Out

Acting out stories helps students focus on what is happening in the story. Choose two students to act out each page. Several pairs of students can join in this activity with each pair acting out an event. You may also have two students pantomime an activity and let other students find the page that the two students are acting out.

Make the Book Available

So that students can enjoy the book repeatedly, place the big book in the Reading Center or put several small-book versions (if you have them) in book buckets. Books that you have read to the class are always favorites for students to read during Self-Selected Reading time. Many students wonder if they can read these books by themselves. Let them have the opportunity to find out! The pictures make pretend reading the book easier for students who are still at that stage.

First-grade reading usually begins with shared reading of big books. The big books you have used and activities you have done for Shared reading will prepare students for beginning-reading instruction in first grade.

Self-Selected Reading

After read-aloud time, let students read on their own for 10–15 minutes from books in the book buckets. **The books that students choose as their favorites are the ones to have available in the buckets, so that students can visit with them one more time before school is out for the summer. Book buckets always contain both fiction and nonfiction titles.** Young students, just like adults, have favorite genres, so some students will prefer one type of book. If you have read a variety of books during read-aloud sessions, then students have been exposed to many types of books and know what they like best.

Students should select their books and either sit in their seats or find comfortable places in the room to read. Remind students to read quietly until they hear the timer go off! Most kindergarten students read with their lips as well as their eyes. Whisper reading helps them comprehend what they are reading but does not disrupt other students' learning.

As you circulate around the room, you will notice that most students are reading. Visit with the few students who need help doing this correctly. As you listen to students read, talk about the books that they have chosen.

- What is happening in the story?

- What does the student think will happen next and why?

- Why did she choose this particular book?

- What other books has the class read that are like this book?

- What other books has the student read by this author?

- What is his favorite part of the book?

- Can the student show you that page?

This one-on-one time with each child is important for beginning readers. It is a time to talk about books with students and assess their decoding and comprehension skills. Don't forget to "Ooh!" and "Aah!" at their reading!

Writing with Students

Predictable Charts

Read *Animal Mothers* and let students tell you what they know about animal mothers and what they do other than carry their babies. At the top of a piece of chart paper, write Happy Mother's Day! Then, let students tell you what they think human mothers do.

Touch Reading

The following day, ask students to touch read their sentences about mothers.

Sentence Builders

The next day, write several sentences from this chart on sentence strips and cut the sentences into words. Let each student be a word in the sentence. Let students find their places and build each sentence. Ask the first student, "Why are you standing at the beginning of the sentence?" See

---

Happy Mother's Day!

Mothers play with you. (Jasmine)

Mothers ride horses with you. (Olivia)

Mothers help you. (Adam)

Mothers cook for you. (Michelle)

Mothers let you have sleepovers. (Emily)

Mothers love you. (Ryan)

Mothers help you clean your room. (William)

Mothers buy you things. (David)

Mothers bake cookies. (Mitchell)

Mothers take you out to eat. (Richard)

Mothers watch TV with you. (Nikki)

Mothers care about you. (Julie)

Mothers read books to you. (Jimmy)

Mothers help you set the table. (Tiara)

Mothers take you to the zoo. (Erica)

Mothers take you to the movies. (Mike)

Mothers take you to baseball practice. (Jacob)

We love our mothers! (Miss Williams)

---

if the first student can tell you that the capital letter at the beginning of her word helped determine where she would stand. Likewise, see if the last student can tell you that the period at the end of his word showed him where to stand. After each sentence is built, read the words aloud so that the rest of the class can check the sentence.

Making a Class Book

After several sentences have been built, have each student cut apart the words in her sentence and put the words in order. Check to see that each word is in the correct place before students paste the words on their papers. Some students may still need help with this, but others find it simple. Finally, have students illustrate their sentences. When checking the sentences, ask, "What will you draw?" Each student should be able to tell you that she will draw a mother doing whatever he said for the predictable chart.

After students have finished illustrating their sentences, help them put the pages of the class book in order. Use the predictable chart to help students. Add front and back covers to the book using construction paper and write the title on the front with a thick black marker. Now, you have another class book to add to your collection. At the very end of the year, give the class-made books to students as souvenirs of their time in kindergarten.

Other Ideas for Predictable Charts

Another book that lends itself to a predictable chart is *When I Grow Up* by Babs Bell Hajdusiewicz (Dominie Press, 1996). This book includes rhythm and rhyme. After enjoying the book for the first reading, reread it and round up the rhymes or write a predictable chart using the sentence "When I grow up, I might . . . . "

Writing by Students
Young Authors' Conference

Share what students write at school each day with their families during a Young Authors' Conference. If you have been saving each student's writing in a journal, folder, or on a disc, you already have the stories. Now, students must decide which ones to publish. **Do not edit students' stories; if you do, many students will not be able to read them.** Typing the stories makes them easier for everyone to read, but print them just as they are.

You have modeled stories and think-alouds each day as you wrote on chart paper. Continue to do this with stories about mothers, fathers, summer, picnics, field trips, end-of-the-year events, and things students learned in kindergarten. As students finish publishing their books, they return to the writing process and write more.

Show students how to make a book. First, cut pieces of plain paper in half. Then, cut a piece of construction paper in half for the front and back covers. Staple or bind the pages and covers together to make a blank book. (Usually, you can find a few parents who will make books for the class.) Neatly print each sentence of a student's story on a different line. If the story is fewer than five sentences, help the student write more sentences. Then, neatly print the story.

My Cat

I play with my cat.

I fed my cat.

My cat jops on the wendo.

My cat jops on my bad.

My cat wach me brsh my teth.

My cat is spashl to me.

Lensi

The Earth

It is so fun piceg up trash.

I want the earth to be clen.

I no that sumwun will halpe me.

If we have trash all over the earth we will not have H2O.

So thats wiy we net to clen up the earth.

Tac car of the earth so anomos can breth.

I glad sombuttle is halpeg me.

I net to clean up the earth.

The earth is still pertey.

Im a pes of the earth.

Adam

Cut out the title and paste it on the title page. Next, cut out each sentence and paste it on a separate page. Put a dedication page (at the beginning) and an About the Author page (at the end) in the book. Then, have the student illustrate her pages. When each student's book is complete, let the student practice reading the book to you and to visiting students from upper-grade classes, if desired. This practice will help students learn to read to their families.

Some teachers have punch and cookies for their Young Authors' Conference or Tea, usually held right before Mother's Day. Sometimes, family members are amazed to see so many kindergarten students writing and reading!

Working with Words

Rhyming Books

Continue to read books that have some rhyming words. Let students listen for the words and point them out when you reread the book. *Hop on Pop* by Dr. Seuss (Random House, 1963) claims that it is "The Simplest Seuss for the Youngest Use." The book is filled with rhyming words and funny pictures. Many students have read this book at home for years and will tell you, "That's a good book!" when you show it to them. One page shows a mouse on a house, and the next page shows a house on a mouse. It has pages with words like **sad**, **dad**, **bad**, and **had**.

> "Dad is sad.
> He is very, very sad.
> He had a bad day.
> What a day Dad had."

Rounding Up the Rhymes

The first reading is to enjoy the book. The second time you read the book, ask students to listen for rhyming words. Talk about the words that rhyme on each page and write them on the board or a chart. Here are some examples from *Hop on Pop*:

up	all	all	day	red
pup	tall	ball	play	bed
cup	small	wall		Ned
		fall		Ed

Ask, "What do you notice about these words?" Can students find the same spelling patterns (called rimes) after the beginning sounds (called onsets)? Can they add rhyming words to this list—**may**, **pay**, **say**, etc.? Students who have been exposed to rhyming words, can hear rhymes, can see the spelling patterns in rhymes, and can add to a list of rhyming words with real or nonsense words have developed the phonemic awareness that is essential to learning how to read.

Clapping Syllables

Clapping syllables helps students listen to words and separate them into beats. Do this activity with summer words, like **swim**, **pool**, **ocean**, **mountains**, **baseball**, **playing**, **book**, **bike**, and **sun**. Write the words on index cards and put them in a pocket chart. Tell students that you will say the words and that they should listen for the beats. Ask students to clap to show how many beats each word has. Say each word. Help students decide that **swim** is a one-beat word and that **ocean** is a two-beat word. Once you have said 10 words, do this again, pointing to the words as you clap the beats. Explain that if a word has more claps, it probably takes more letters to write.

Making Words

During this last month and a half of kindergarten, do Making Words lessons with the long vowel patterns **ay**, **ake**, **ate**, **ame**, **eat**, **ide**, and the familiar patterns **all** and **ook** that are hard to explain. Tell students what the pattern says rather than blending letters together like you have been doing for the previous patterns.

Remember the steps for Making Words lessons in kindergarten are:

1. Read a book with the selected pattern in the title and/or in the book.

2. Make and read some words with the pattern.

3. Decide what letters to use with the pattern to spell some words. Have students point to each needed letter and have the student with that letter join the other letter students.

Here are the books and words you need for each pattern.

Making Words Lessons

Pattern: ay
Letters: a y d h l M p r s t w
Book to Read:
Annie Bananie by Leah Komaiko (HarperTrophy, 1987)
Read the book. Reread pages 8–9. Talk about the **ay** pattern in **play** and **away**.
Words to Make and Spell: day, hay, lay, May, pay, ray, say, way, stay, tray

Pattern: ake
Letters: a k e b c f J l m r s t w
Book to Read:
Jake Baked the Cake by B. G. Hennessy (Puffin, 1992)
Read the book. Reread, "While Jake baked the cake" on several pages. Talk about the **ake** pattern.
Words to Make and Spell: bake, cake, Jake, lake, fake, make, rake, sake, take, wake, stake, brake

Pattern: ate
Letters: a t e d g h K k l m N r s
Book to Read:
The Wedding by Eve Bunting (Charlesbridge, 2005)
Read the book. Reread page 8. Talk about the **ate** pattern in **gate**, **date**, and **late**.
Words to Make and Spell: date, gate, hate, Kate, late, mate, Nate, rate, skate, slate

Pattern: ame

Letters: a m e b f l n s t

Book to Read:

Loud Lips Lucy by Tolya L. Thompson (Savor Publishing House, 2002)

Read the book. Reread the tenth page (pages are not numbered). Talk about the **ame** pattern in **name** and **same**.

Words to Make and Spell: fame, name, same, tame, blame

Pattern: eat

Letters: e a t b h m n s

Book to Read:

How I Spent My Summer Vacation by Mark Teague (Dragonfly Books, 1995)

Read the book. Reread page 23. Talk about the **eat** pattern in **eat** and **beat**.

Words to Make and Spell: beat, heat, meat, neat, seat

Pattern: ide

Letters: i d e b h l r s t w

Book to Read:

Inside Outside Upside Down by Jan Berenstain and Stan Berenstain (Random House, 1968)

Read the book. Talk about the **ide** pattern in the title words **inside**, **outside**, and **upside**.

Words to Make and Spell: hide, ride, side, wide, tide, bride, slide

Pattern: all

Letters: a l l b c f h m s t w

Book to Read:

The Cat in the Hat by Dr. Seuss (Random House, 1957)

Read the book. Reread page 40. Talk about the **all** pattern in **hall** and **wall**.

Words to Make and Spell: ball, call, fall, hall, mall, tall, wall, small, stall

Pattern: ook

Letters: o o k b c h l n r s t

Book to Read:

One Fish Two Fish Red Fish Blue Fish by Dr. Seuss (Random House, 1960)

Read the book. Reread pages 30–31. Talk about the **ook** pattern in **hook**, **book**, **cook**, and **look**.

Words to Make and Spell: book, cook, hook, look, nook, took, brook, shook

Environmental Print: Restaurants

Focus on environmental print in May and June so that students can look for words and letters they know over the summer. Students need to practice at home some of the things they do in school. One way to make sure that they can do this is to use environmental print. Students practiced letter names with cereal boxes last month. This month, focus on fast-food restaurants. It is hard to drive in any city or town without seeing these restaurant signs. The bags and food wrappers also advertise the restaurant's name and the products it sells.

Talk about the restaurants that students visit. Bring in bags or food wrappers with these logos and names on them. Most kindergarten students can read the logos of their favorite restaurants. Graph their favorites and see which restaurants are the most popular for students. Talk about these restaurants, discussing a different one each day.

For example, if BURGER KING® is the favorite fast-food restaurant, start with it. Hold up a BURGER KING® bag, and have students look at it. Talk about the colors and the pictures on the bag. What does the logo have to do with the restaurant name? Have students count the letters in **BURGER KING**® with you: "1–2–3–4–5–6–space–7–8–9–10. There are 10 letters." Then, have students say the letter names with you ("B–U–R–G–E–R–space–K–I–N–G").

Next, pass out laminated letter cards. The letters should be identical to the letters on the bag or logo. Ask, "Who has the B? U? R? G? E? R? Space? K? I? N? G?" Have students stand in order to spell **BURGER KING**®. As you point to each child with a letter card, have the student say her letter. Then, collect the letters and have students return to their seats.

Put the letters in the pocket chart and hold up the bag again. Ask students "What do you notice about the words **BURGER KING**®?" You may hear responses like the following:

"All of the letters are capital."

"The bag is white."

"It begins with **B**, like **Bobby** or **Barbara**."

"**BURGER KING**® is two words."

"You can hear the **k** sound at the beginning of **KING**."

"There are two **r**'s in **BURGER KING**®."

After discussing the words **BURGER KING**®, the logo, and the letters in the two words, let students look at the laminated letters in the pocket chart. Have them write the words **BURGER KING**® on pieces of drawing paper with their black crayons or markers. Then, have students draw a picture of the restaurant, the logo, or the foods served at the restaurant.

Once you have done this activity with several restaurants, students will have another way to practice letter names at home. Students enjoy showing what they have learned in school, and environmental print gives them that opportunity each day even if they do not come from homes with books and magazines.

Note: The brand name used in the previous exercise is not owned by or affiliated with Carson-Dellosa Publishing Company, Inc., in any way and is used for illustrative purposes only. Burger King Corporation is the exclusive license of the registered Burger King and Bun Halves Logo trademarks.

Centers

Reading Center

Each center has a task for students. Students get to practice reading and writing for real reasons as they read the signs in the centers and perform these tasks. Each week, find tasks to enhance the themes. Planting and flowers are one theme in May/June; Mother's Day is another. The centers are tied closely to the themes and signs. Books on summer, travel folders and brochures, favorite books read during kindergarten, and a lot of beginning readers are found in the Reading Center.

Writing Center

The May Picture Dictionary chart or bulletin board has words that students want to write about at this time of year. You might want to put some materials in the Writing Center for students to make journals to take home for summer writing. The computer is still popular with students when they go to the Writing Center. You will notice that some students write longer stories when they have the help of a computer.

Restaurants Center

Since most kindergartners are familiar with restaurants, add a Restaurant Center in May and show how people read and write as they work. In this center, put menus, signs on the wall, order pads, tables, chairs, place mats, plates, utensils, play food, play credit cards, play money, play checks, and a cash register. Someone could be the cook reading orders and preparing the food. Someone could be the waiter or waitress writing the order. You need a lot of customers to read the menu, place their orders, and pay for their food.

Assessing Progress

To determine how various students are developing in their reading, writing, and word knowledge, teachers need to be keen observers of students. The most practical diagnostic tool for this purpose is Marie Clay's *An Observation Survey of Early Literacy Achievement* (Heinemann, 1997). The survey, first developed as a screening device for Reading Recovery, has been adapted for classroom use. This survey is a valid and authentic measure of students' emergent literacy behaviors and may become a part of kindergarten assessment.

Many teachers have come up with their own ways of observing students' early reading and writing progress. Here are some behaviors to observe as you assess student development, as listed by Patricia Cunningham in *Phonics They Use: Words for Reading and Writing* (Longman, 2000):

• Students read or pretend read favorite books, poems, songs, and chants.

• Students write in whatever ways they can, and they can read what they wrote even if no one else can.

• Students track print—they point to the words using left-to-right/top-to-bottom conventions.

• Students know critical jargon—they can point to just one word, the first word in a sentence, just one letter, the first letter in a word, the longest word, etc.

• Students recognize and can write some concrete words: their names and names of other students, days of the week, and favorite words from books, poems, and chants.

• Students demonstrate phonemic awareness, orally manipulating words by taking off letters and changing the first letters to make words rhyme.

• Students recognize words that rhyme and can make up rhymes.

• Students can name many letters and can tell you words that begin with common initial sounds.

• Students are learning more about the world in which they live and are able to talk about what they know.

• Students can listen to stories and informational books and retell the most important information. They see themselves as readers, writers, and new members of the "literacy club."

Many students have hundreds of hours of literacy interactions at home during which they develop understandings critical to their success in beginning reading. **Our school programs must be structured in a way that provide those experiences and interactions (that some students have already had) for all students.** This will not be an easy task. Schools do not have the luxury of providing these learning experiences one student at a time, but teachers can offer literacy learning in ways that closely simulate these home experiences.

Critical Understandings That Are the Building Blocks to Success

The multilevel reading and writing activities presented in this book are the building blocks to success for all kindergarten students. When understood and applied in the classroom, these critical understandings will be observed in young learners:

1. Students learn that reading provides enjoyment and information, and they develop the desire to learn how to read and write.

2. Students learn many new concepts and add words and meanings to their speaking vocabularies.

3. Students learn print concepts, including to read words from left to right and to read a page from top to bottom.

4. Students develop phonemic awareness, including the concept of rhyme.

5. Students learn how to read and write some interesting-to-them-words.

6. Students learn some letter names and sounds that are usually connected to interesting words they have learned.

In developmentally appropriate kindergarten classrooms, teachers provide a variety of experiences so that all students develop these critical understandings that are the building blocks to success!

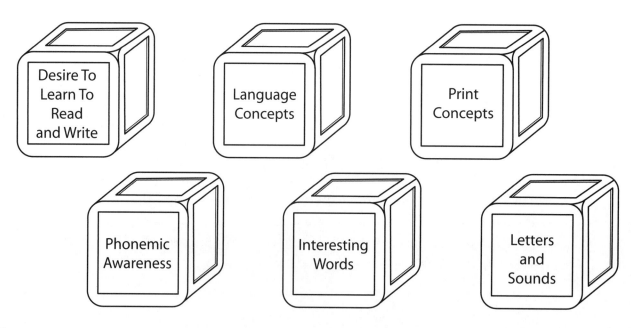

Desire To Learn To Read and Write

Language Concepts

Print Concepts

Phonemic Awareness

Interesting Words

Letters and Sounds

The Research Base for
Month-by-Month Phonics

The *Month-by-Month Phonics* books for each grade level contain a variety of motivating, multilevel activities. These activities are also research-based. Research reviews (National Reading Panel, 2000; Stahl, Duffy-Hester, and Stahl, 1998) have suggested that the most effective phonics instruction is explicit, planned and sequential, and systematic. *Month-by-Month Phonics* meets all of these criteria.

Month-by-Month Phonics Is Explicit

It is generally agreed that phonics instruction can be explicit or implicit. Adams (1990) defines explicit phonics as "the provision of systematic instruction on the relation of letter-sounds to words" (p. 49). She defines implicit phonics as "the philosophy of letting students induce letter-sounds from whole words" (p. 49). *Month-by-Month Phonics* is not an implicit phonics program that expects students to "induce letter-sounds from whole words." At all levels of the program, students are explicitly taught letter-sound relationships and how these relationships transfer to decoding and spelling unfamiliar words. In kindergarten, students learn letter names and letter sounds and are expected to begin using letter sounds during shared reading and writing before they are taught any sight words. In first grade, students learn the most common consonant and vowel patterns and apply these to decoding and spelling words. In second grade, the focus is on less-common vowel patterns and all of the patterns taught in first grade are reviewed. Students also learn that some vowels have two or more common patterns and learn to distinguish these as they read and write words in Reading/Writing Rhymes lessons. In third grade, students continue to work with complex vowel patterns and are taught explicitly how to combine their visual checking with vowel patterns to spell words correctly in an activity called What Looks Right? Common prefixes and suffixes are taught, and students learn to use these morphemic parts to decode, spell, and access meanings for polysyllabic words. This emphasis on using morphemic parts to decode, spell, and build meaning for polysyllabic words is continued in the upper grades as students use roots, prefixes, and suffixes to unlock thousands of polysyllabic words. Explicit instruction of English spelling patterns is evident in all of the *Month-by-Month Phonics* activities. More importantly, perhaps, students are explicitly taught how to use letter patterns to actually decode and spell new words when they are reading and writing.

Month-by-Month Phonics Is Planned and Sequential

It is generally agreed that phonics instruction can be planned and sequential or provided as the need arises. According to the Learning First Alliance (2000):

> "Embedded and incidental phonics are characterized by an implicit approach in which teachers do not use phonics elements in a planned sequence to guide instruction but instead find opportunities to highlight particular phonics elements when they appear in text."

Research Base ···

When the chair of the National Reading Panel testified on its findings before a congressional subcommittee, he said:

> "The greatest improvements were seen from systematic phonics instruction. This type of phonics instruction consists of teaching a planned sequence of phonics elements, rather than highlighting elements as they happen to appear in a text." (Langenberg, 2000)

The instruction in *Month-by-Month Phonics* is not embedded, incidental, or implicit, and it does not wait to "highlight elements as they happen to appear in a text." Rather, it is planned and sequential, because during each month at each grade, there is a planned sequence of lessons with specific letters, sounds, and words provided for the teacher to use. In the program, students begin by learning phonemic awareness, letter names, and letter sounds. They progress to learning digraphs, blends, and vowel patterns in one- and two-syllable words. They continue to progress to decode and spell polysyllabic words.

In addition to being planned and sequential, *Month-by-Month Phonics* is also multilevel. While targeting specific phonics/spelling elements, each lesson also provides opportunities for students to learn a variety of important insights about letters and sounds—including some that are easier than the lesson focus and some that go beyond the focus.

In every Making Words lesson for grades 1–3, students are encouraged to stretch out words and put the letters together to form words—an activity that helps students develop the segmenting and blending phonemic-awareness skills. The words made in the middle part of a Making Words lesson contain the targeted phonics/spelling element. The first words in each lesson, however, are easier words and allow students to review or relearn previously taught patterns. The last words in every Making Words lesson—including the secret word that can be made with all of the letters—are more challenging words and are included to provide opportunities for advanced students to extend their knowledge of letters and sounds. When teachers sort words in a Making Words lesson, they sort on a variety of levels. Sorting out words that share a root, prefix, or suffix helps students begin to pay attention to these important morphemic parts, even before that becomes a major focus of instruction. Words can also be sorted by beginning letters to support the development of that knowledge for students who haven't quite mastered it yet. Teachers always sort for rhyming words and transfer those rhyming patterns to decode and spell new words. Sorting words and decoding and spelling new words allows all students to notice a variety of patterns and move forward in their understanding of how the English alphabetic system works. Throughout the program, teachers are reminded of how the activities are designed to be multilevel and how to maximize the effectiveness of the activities for students at all different levels of understanding about words.

The National Reading Panel report did not offer any research-based solutions to the problem of students being at different levels in their word knowledge, but the report did acknowledge the universality of the problem and the dilemma all teachers face.

"As with any instructional program, there is always the question: 'Does one size fit all?' Teachers may be expected to use a particular phonics program with their class, yet it quickly becomes apparent that the program suits some students more than others. In the early grades, students are known to vary greatly in the skills they bring to school. There will be some students who already know the letter–sound correspondences, some students who can decode words, and others who have little or no knowledge. Should teachers proceed through the program and ignore these students?" (p. 2-136)

Month-by-Month Phonics is planned and sequential—and multilevel! Each lesson has a focus but also provides something for both late bloomers and early developers. One size never fits all, and teachers must find ways to accommodate the wide range of learners in their classrooms. *Month-by-Month Phonics* provides teachers with the help needed to accomplish this goal.

Month-by-Month Phonics Is Systematic

It is generally agreed that phonics instruction can be systematic or unsystematic. Adams contrasts "systematic phonics instruction" with "emphasis on connected reading and meaning" (p. 42) and with "meaning emphasis, language instruction, and connected reading" (p. 49). The instruction in *Month-by-Month Phonics* is systematic because a separate time slot is set aside each day for teaching phonics. During this time, the focus is on phonics and word study, rather than on the other essential components of a comprehensive literacy program. The instruction in *Month-by-Month Phonics* is also systematic because it includes regular guidance for the teacher in how to coach students to apply the phonics they are learning during connected reading and writing.

What does the research say about the form that systematic phonics instruction should take? Again, we turn to the National Reading Panel report and to Stahl et al. for guidance. The National Reading Panel report (2000) concluded the following:

"In teaching phonics explicitly and systematically, several different instructional approaches have been used. These include synthetic phonics, analytic phonics, embedded phonics, analogy phonics, onset-rime phonics, and phonics through spelling . . . Phonics-through-spelling programs teach students to transform sounds into letters to write words. Phonics in context approaches teach students to use sound-letter correspondences along with context clues to identify unfamiliar words they encounter in text. Analogy phonics programs teach students to use parts of written words they already know to identify new words. The distinctions between systematic phonics approaches are not absolute, however, and some phonics programs combine two or more of these types of instruction." (p. 2-89)

The National Reading Panel report (2000) went on to conclude the following:

"Specific systematic phonics programs are all more effective than non-phonics programs and they do not appear to differ significantly from each other in their effectiveness." (p. 2-132)

Research Base ···

Stahl, Duffy-Hester, and Stahl (1998) discuss two kinds of "early and systematic phonics instruction" (p. 344): traditional and contemporary. Making Words, one of the main kinds of phonics instruction in *Month-by-Month Phonics*, was included by Stahl et al. (1998) in the "contemporary" kind of systematic phonics instruction. The National Reading Panel report (2000) cautioned its readers not to conclude that newer phonics instructional programs are inferior to the ones examined in the report's meta-analyses:

> "Most of these [phonics instructional] programs were developed over 20 years ago, providing researchers with more time to study them than recently developed programs. . . . [T]here was no reason to expect these [older] programs to be more effective than [newer] programs not in the set being compared." (p. 2-105)

Some people associate systematic phonics instruction with decodable text, because many synthetic forms of systematic phonics instruction include decodable text. The National Reading Panel (2000) did not conclude that phonics instruction must have decodable text in order to be considered systematic. Rather, the panel concluded that research does not support the need for decodable text when teaching systematic phonics:

> "Very little research has attempted to determine whether the use of decodable books in systematic phonics programs has any influence on the progress that some or all students make in learning to read." (p. 2-137)

Recently, questions have been raised again about the best format in which to deliver phonics instruction. The National Reading Panel report (2000) reviewed research on this question and concluded the following:

> "Systematic phonics instruction is effective when delivered through tutoring, through small groups, and through teaching classes of students . . . All effect sizes were statistically greater than zero, and no one differed significantly from the others." (p. 2-93)

The Type of Systematic Phonics Instruction in *Month-by-Month Phonics*

The National Reading Panel (2000) described several different types of effective phonics instruction, including analogy phonics, onset-rime phonics, phonics through spelling, and phonics in context. *Month-by-Month Phonics* combines all of these types of phonics instruction.

Analogy and Onset-Rime Phonics

Both analogy and onset-rime phonics programs teach students to use parts of written words they already know to identify new words. The parts used are the beginning letters (onsets) and the rhyming pattern (rimes). Cunningham did some of the original research that resulted in the *Month-by-Month Phonics* activities early in her career (Cunningham, 1975–1976; 1979; 1980; 1992; Cunningham and Guthrie, 1982). In this research, analogy-based decoding strategies were investigated and found to be effective in teaching students to decode words. Recently, several research reviews have affirmed analogy strategies, along with other strategies, as effective ways to teach decoding.

In onset-rime phonics, readers decode and spell a word by dividing the word between the onset and rime, pronouncing both chunks, and blending these two pronunciations together. In analogy phonics, students decode and spell new words by thinking of known words with similar patterns. Here is an example of how these two decoding strategies might work:

Imagine a reader who comes upon the word **primp** for the first time. If this reader knows the sounds usually associated with **pr** and **imp**, she will blend the sounds of these two chunks together to pronounce the word. She has decoded the new word, **primp**, by dividing between the onset, **pr**, and the rime, **imp**, pronouncing these two chunks, and recombining them to produce the word.

Now, imagine another reader encountering the word **primp** for the first time. This reader also divides between the onset and the rime and thinks of the pronunciation for **pr**, but this reader doesn't have a pronunciation stored for the **imp** rime. This reader then does a quick search through his word store for words he knows that have the **imp** rime. He thinks of **shrimp** and **chimp** and uses these two known words with the same rime to pronounce the **imp** rime. He then blends the onset, **pr**, with the rime, **imp**, and pronounces the word **primp**. Analogies are likenesses or similarities. When teachers ask students to think of analogous situations, teachers are asking them to think of similar situations. When students decode words by analogy, they use similar words to generate pronunciations for new words.

Many of the activities in *Month-by-Month Phonics* focus students' attention on the onsets and rimes in words and how they can use these to decode and spell new words. During these activities, students learn to use both onset-rime phonics and analogy phonics.

During Making Words lesson in grades 1–3, the first part of the lesson, in which students combine letters to spell words, incorporates a spelling approach to phonics. The Sort and Transfer steps of a Making Words lesson incorporate onset-rime and analogy phonics. Words are sorted according to their rimes into rhyming words. Students are then shown new words that have the same rimes as some of the sorted words. They use the sorted words to pronounce new words with the same rimes. To show students how to use rimes to spell words, the teacher pronounces two words that rhyme with some of the sorted words, and students spell the new words using the patterns from the sorted words.

Three other activities used in *Month-by-Month Phonics* also teach students how to use the onset-rime- and analogy-decoding strategies. In grades 1–3, students use onset and rime patterns to decode and spell new words in Rounding Up the Rhymes, Reading/Writing Rhymes, and Using Words You Know.

Phonics through Spelling

Phonics-through-spelling programs teach students to transform sounds into letters to write words. Making Words, one of the main kinds of phonics instruction in *Month-by-Month Phonics*, was included by Stahl, Duffy-Hester, and Stahl (1998) in the contemporary kind of systematic phonics instruction that they called a "spelling-based approach." During the first step of a Making Words lesson, students manipulate letters to spell words called out by the teacher. This is clearly a spelling-based approach to decoding.

Research Base ··

In addition to providing students with a spelling-based approach to decoding, every Making Words lesson helps students develop phonemic awareness. **Phonemic awareness** is the ability to mentally manipulate sounds in words, to hear when words rhyme and create rhymes, to segment words into sounds, and to blend those sounds back together to form words. During Making Words activities, students are encouraged to stretch out words and explicitly represent each phoneme they hear with a letter, from left-to-right, through the word. Because these activities teach students to hear the phonemes in words, use letters, and add, delete, and replace letters to spell different words, they also teach phonemic awareness in a way that is consistent with another conclusion of the National Reading Panel (2000):

> "Instruction that taught phoneme manipulation with letters helped normally developing readers and at–risk readers acquire PA [phonemic awareness] better than PA instruction without letters." (p. 2-4)

Other activities used in *Month-by-Month Phonics* can also be classified as spelling-based approaches. These include Changing a Hen to a Fox, Word Sorting and Hunting, and What Looks Right? in grades 1–3.

Phonics in Context

Phonics-in-context approaches teach students to use letter-sound correspondences and context clues to identify unfamiliar words they encounter in text. Using knowledge of beginning-letter (onset) sounds and context is the major purpose of a *Month-by-Month Phonics* activity, Guess the Covered Word. In this activity, students are presented with sentences and paragraphs in which some words have been covered. They guess what each word is without being able to see any of the letters. Next, the teacher uncovers the beginning letters—all of the letters up to the first vowel. Students now guess words that make sense and have all of the correct beginning letters. Students quickly learn that just guessing at a word is not a very productive strategy but that using both the context and all of the beginning letters will often allow them to come up with the correct word.

Research Supporting *Month-by-Month Phonics* Activities

Since the publication of the Stahl et. al and National Reading Panel research reviews, several studies have been published that support the kind of systematic phonics instruction in *Month-by-Month Phonics*. Davis (2000) found that spelling-based decoding instruction was as effective as reading-based decoding instruction for all of her students but was more effective for students with poor phonological awareness. Juel and Minden-Cupp (2000) observed that the most effective teachers of students who entered first grade with few literacy skills combined systematic letter-sound instruction with onset-rime/analogy instruction and taught these units to apply in both reading and writing. McCandliss, Beck, Sandak, and Perfetti (2003) investigated the effectiveness of Beck's instructional strategy, Word Building, with students who had failed to benefit from traditional phonics instruction. Word Building is very similar to Making Words, Changing a Hen into a Fox, and Reading/Writing Rhymes, three of the phonics instructional activities in *Month-by-Month Phonics*. These researchers found that students who received this word-building instruction demonstrated significantly greater improvements on standardized measures of decoding, reading comprehension, and phonological awareness.

Conclusion

All of the activities in *Month-by-Month Phonics* are supported by research, and the program is explicit, planned and sequential, and systematic. Unlike some other explicit, planned and sequential, and systematic phonics instruction, the instruction in *Month-by-Month Phonics* has variety, is multilevel to meet the needs of a range of learners, and is motivating for students. The instruction in *Month-by-Month Phonics* is consistent with the conclusion of Stahl, Duffy-Hester, and Stahl (1998) in their review of phonics research:

> "Good phonics instruction should not teach rules, need not use worksheets, should not dominate instruction, and does not have to be boring." (p. 341)

References

Children's Books Cited

A Is for Africa by Ifeoma Onyefulu (Puffin, 1997)

A Is for Animals: An ABC Pop-Up by David Pelham (Little Simon, 1991)

A My Name Is Alice by Jane Bayer (Puffin, 1984)

A You're Adorable by Buddy Kaye, Fred Wise, and Sidney Lippman (Candlewick, 1996)

ABC and You by Eugenie Fernandes (Penguin Putnam, 1990)

ABC I Like Me! by Nancy Carlson (Puffin, 1997)

The Accidental Zucchini: An Unexpected Alphabet by Max Grover (Voyager Books, 1993)

Airplanes by Lola M. Schaefer (Bridgestone, 1999)

Alexander and the Terrible, Horrible, No Good, Very Bad Day by Judith Viorst (Aladdin, 1972)

Alexander, Who's Not (Do You Hear Me? I Mean It!) Going to Move by Judith Viorst (Aladdin, 1995)

All Aboard ABC by Douglas Magee and Robert Newman (Puffin, 1990)

All About Seeds by Susan Kuchalla (Troll Communications, 1982)

Alphabatics by Suse MacDonald (Aladdin, 1986)

Alphabet City by Stephen T. Johnson (Puffin, 1995)

An Alphabet Salad: Fruits and Vegetables from A to Z by Sarah L. Schuette (Capstone Press, 2003)

The Alphabet Tale by Jan Garten (Greenwillow, 1994)

Amazing Airplanes by Tony Mitton and Ant Parker (Kingfisher, 2002)

Animal ABCs by Susan Hood (Troll Communications, 1997)

Animal Mothers by Atsushi Komori (Houghton Mifflin, 1996)

Animal Parade by Jakki Wood (Scholastic, 1994)

Animals in Winter by Henrietta Bancroft and Richard G. Van Gelder (HarperTrophy, 1996)

Annie Bananie by Leah Komaiko (HarperTrophy, 1987)

Ants by Cheryl Coughlan (Capstone Press, 1999)

Ape in a Cape: An Alphabet of Odd Animals by Fritz Eichenberg (Voyager, 1952)

Are You My Mother? by P. D. Eastman (Random House, 1960)

Arthur's Valentine by Marc Brown (Little, Brown Young Readers, 1980)

Babies on the Go by Linda Ashman (Harcourt Children's Books, 2003)

Bad Kitty by Nick Bruel (Roaring Brook Press, 2005)

Bear Snores On by Karma Wilson (Margaret K. McElderry, 2002)

Bear Stays Up for Christmas by Karma Wilson (Margaret K. McElderry, 2004)

Beetles by Cheryl Coughlan (Capstone Press, 1999)

Berenstain Bears Go to Camp by Stan Berenstain and Jan Berenstain (Random House, 1982)

The Best Thing About Valentines by Eleanor Hudson (Cartwheel, 2004)

Bicycles by Lola M. Schaefer (Heinemann, 2003)

The Biggest Valentine Ever by Steven Kroll (Cartwheel, 2006)

The Brand New Kid by Katie Couric (Doubleday, 2000)

Bread and Jam for Frances by Russell Hoban (HarperTrophy, 1993)

Bright Eyes, Brown Skin by Cheryl Willis Hudson and Bernette G. Ford (Just Us Books, 1990)

Brown Bear, Brown Bear, What Do You See? by Bill Martin Jr. (Henry Holt and Company, 1967)

A Bug in a Jug and Other Funny Rhymes by Gloria Patrick (Scholastic, 1970)

Bugs, Bugs, Bugs! by Jennifer Dussling (DK Children, 1999)

Bumble Bees by Cheryl Coughlan (Capstone Press, 2000)

Busy Boats by Tony Mitton and Ant Parker (Kingfisher, 2002)

A Busy Year by Leo Lionni (Scholastic, 1993)

Cable Cars by Lola M. Schaefer (Bridgestone, 1999)

Calendar by Myra Cohn Livingston (Holiday House, 2007)

Caps for Sale: A Tale of a Peddler, Some Monkeys and Their Monkey Business by Esphyr Slobodkina (HarperTrophy, 1940)

The Carrot Seed by Ruth Krauss (HarperCollins, 1945)

References ···

The Cat in the Hat by Dr. Seuss (Random House, 1957)

Cats by Helen Frost (Capstone Press, 2001)

Celebrate Hanukkah: With Light, Latkes, and Dreidels by Deborah Heiligman (National Geographic Children's Books, 2006)

A Chair for My Mother by Vera Williams (HarperTrophy, 1984)

Chicken Soup with Rice: A Book of Months by Maurice Sendak (HarperTrophy, 1962)

Chickens on the Go! by Judith A. McEwen (www.chickensonthego.com, 2006)

A Child's Year by Joan Walsh Anglund (Golden Books, 1992)

Christmas Time by Gail Gibbons (Holiday House, 1982)

City Mouse–Country Mouse and Two More Mouse Tales from Aesop by Aesop (Scholastic, 1987)

Clifford the Big Red Dog by Norman Bridwell (Cartwheel, 1985)

Clifford's First Valentine's Day by Norman Bridwell (Cartwheel, 1997)

Color Dance by Ann Jonas (Greenwillow Books, 1989)

The Complete Adventures of Curious George by Margret Rey and H. A. Rey (Houghton Mifflin, 1941)

Cool Cars by Tony Mitton and Ant Parker (Kingfisher, 2002)

Corduroy's Christmas by Don Freeman and B. G. Hennessy (Scholastic, 1993)

Country Fair by Gail Gibbons (Little, Brown and Company, 1994)

Crabby Cat's Party by Joy Cowley (Dominie Press, 2004)

Crickets by Cheryl Coughlan (Capstone Press, 1999)

David McPhail's Animals A to Z by David McPhail (Scholastic, 1989)

Dazzling Diggers by Tony Mitton and Ant Parker (Kingfisher, 2000)

Dibble and Dabble by Dave Saunders and Julie Saunders (Simon and Schuster Children's Publishing, 1990)

Dinosaurs Divorce: A Guide for Changing Families by Laurene Krasny Brown and Marc Brown (Little, Brown Young Readers, 1986)

Does a Kangaroo Have a Mother, Too? by Eric Carle (HarperTrophy, 2000)

Dragonflies by Cheryl Coughlan (Capstone Press, 2000)

Dr. Seuss's ABC by Dr. Seuss (Random House, 1963)

Each Peach Pear Plum by Janet Ahlberg and Allan Ahlberg (Puffin, 1978)

The Ear Book by Al Perkins (Random House, 1968)

Eating the Alphabet: Fruits and Vegetables from A to Z by Lois Ehlert (Harcourt, 1989)

Eeny, Meeny, Miney Mouse by Gwen Pascoe (Educational Insights, 1987)

Emma Kate by Patricia Polacco (Scholastic, 2005)

Everette Anderson's Nine Months Long by Lucille Clifton (Henry Holt and Company, 1988)

Ferries by Lola M. Schaefer (Bridgestone, 2000)

First Snow by Emily Arnold McCully (HarperCollins, 1985)

Five Little Monkeys Jumping on the Bed by Eileen Christelow (Clarion, 1989)

Flashing Fire Engines by Tony Mitton and Ant Parker (Kingfisher, 2000)

Flies by Cheryl Coughlan (Capstone Press, 1999)

The Foot Book by Dr. Seuss (Random House, 1968)

Fox in Socks by Dr. Seuss (Random House, 1965)

Franklin Goes to School by Paulette Bourgeois (Scholastic, 1995)

Franklin's Valentine's Day by Paulette Bourgeois (Scholastic, 1999)

Fred and Ted Go Camping by Peter Eastman (Random House, 2005)

Frederick by Leo Lionni (Pantheon, 1967)

Freight Train by Donald Crews (Greenwillow Books, 1978)

From Acorn to Zoo and Everything in Between in Alphabetical Order by Satoshi Kitamusa (Farrar, Straus and Giroux, 1992)

From Head to Toe by Eric Carle (HarperTrophy, 2007)

The Gingerbread Man by Brenda Parkes and Judith Smith (Mimosa Publications, 2001)

Go, Dog, Go! by P. D. Eastman (Random House, 1961)

Golden Bear by Ruth Young (Puffin, 1994)

Goldilocks and the Three Bears by David McPhail (Cartwheel, 1995)

References ···

Goodnight Moon by Margaret Wise Brown (HarperTrophy, 2007)

Grandma's Helper by Lois Meyer (Pearson, 1993)

Grasshoppers by Cheryl Coughlan (Capstone Press, 1999)

Green Eggs and Ham by Dr. Seuss (Random House, 1960)

The Green Queen by Nick Sharratt (Candlewick, 1992)

Gretchen Groundhog It's Your Day by Abby Levine (Albert Whitman & Company, 1998)

Growing Colors by Bruce McMillan (HarperTrophy, 1994)

Growing Vegetable Soup by Lois Ehlert (Harcourt, 1987)

Guess How Much I Love You by Sam McBratney (Candlewick, 1994)

The Gunnywolf by A. Delaney (HarperCollins, 1992)

Halloween by Miriam Nerlove (Albert Whitman & Company, 1987)

The Happy Hedgehog by Marcus Pfister (North-South Books, 2000)

Harold and the Purple Crayon by Crockett Johnson (HarperTrophy, 1955)

Hattie and the Fox by Mem Fox (Aladdin, 1988)

Haunted House by Bill Martin Jr. (Harcourt, 1970)

Have You Seen My Cat? by Eric Carle (Aladdin, 1988)

Hello, Snow! by Wendy Cheyette Lewison (Grosset & Dunlap, 1994)

Hop on Pop by Dr. Seuss (Random House, 1963)

Horton Hatches the Egg by Dr. Seuss (Random House, 1940)

How Do Apples Grow? by Betsy Maestro (HarperTrophy, 1993)

How I Spent My Summer Vacation by Mark Teague (Dragonfly Books, 1995)

Hunky Dory Ate It by Katie Evans (Puffin, 1992)

I Ain't Gonna Paint No More by Karen Beaumont (Harcourt Children's Books, 2005)

I Am Special by Kimberly Jordano (Creative Teaching Press, 1996)

I Can Read with My Eyes Shut! by Dr. Seuss (Random House, 1978)

I Just Forgot by Mercer Mayer (Random House, 1999)

I Know an Old Lady Who Swallowed a Fly: A Traditional Rhyme by Slug Signorino (Diane Publishing Company, 1993)

I Like the Rain by Claude Belanger (Shortland, 1988)

I Love Cats by Barney Saltzberg (Candlewick, 2005)

I Love Trains! by Philemon Sturges (HarperCollins, 2001)

If You're Happy and You Know It! by Jane Cabrera (Holiday House, 2005)

I'm Sorry by Mercer Mayer (Golden Books, 2000)

In a People House by Dr. Seuss (Random House, 1972)

The Incredible Book Eating Boy by Oliver Jeffers (Philomel Books, 2007)

Inside Outside Upside Down by Jan Berenstain and Stan Berenstain (Random House, 1968)

It Begins with an A by Stephanie Calmenson (Hyperion, 1994)

It Looked Like Spilt Milk by Charles G. Shaw (HarperTrophy, 1988)

It's Pumpkin Time by Zoe Hall (Scholastic, 1994)

It's Spring by Else Holmelund Minarik (Greenwillow, 1989)

I Was So Mad by Mercer Mayer (Random House, 2000)

I Went Walking by Sue Williams (Scholastic, 1989)

I Wish That I Had Duck Feet by Dr. Seuss (Random House, 1965)

Jake Baked the Cake by B. G. Hennessy (Puffin, 1992)

Johnny Appleseed by Steven Kellogg (Scholastic, 1989)

Just Go to Bed by Mercer Mayer (Random House, 2001)

Just Grandma and Me by Mercer Mayer (Random House, 2001)

Just Grandpa and Me by Mercer Mayer (Random House, 2001)

Just Like Daddy by Frank Asch (Aladdin, 1981)

Just Me and My Dad by Mercer Mayer (Random House, 2001)

Just Me and My Mom by Mercer Mayer (Random House, 2001)

Just Me and My Puppy by Mercer Mayer (Random House, 1998)

References ···

Just Me in the Tub by Mercer Mayer (Random House, 2001)

Just a Mess by Mercer Mayer (Random House, 2000)

Just a New Neighbor by Gina Mayer and Mercer Mayer (Golden Books, 2000)

Just a Snowy Vacation by Gina Mayer (Golden Books, 2001)

K Is for Kiss Good Night: A Bedtime Alphabet by Jill Sardegna (Random House, 1994)

Katy and the Big Snow by Virginia Lee Burton (Houghton Mifflin, 1971)

Kindergarten Kids by Ellen Sensi (Scholastic, 1994)

Koala Lou by Mem Fox (Voyager, 1988)

Ladybugs by Cheryl Coughlan (Capstone Press, 2000)

Ladybugs and Other Insects by Gallimard Jeunesse (Scholastic, 2007)

The Lamb and the Butterfly by Arnold Sundgaard (Scholastic, 1988)

Lilly's Chocolate Heart by Kevin Henkes (HarperCollins, 2003)

The Little Engine That Could by Watty Piper (Grosset & Dunlap, 1930)

The Little Red Hen by Byron Barton (HarperTrophy, 1996)

The Little Red Hen by Paul Galdone (Clarion, 1996)

The Little Red Hen by Lucinda McQueen (Scholastic, 1985)

The Little Red Hen: An Old Story by Margot Zemarch (Farrar, Straus and Giroux, 1993)

Look What I Can Do by Jose Aruego (Aladdin, 1971)

Loud Lips Lucy by Tolya L. Thompson (Savor Publishing House, 2002)

Mama, Do You Love Me? by Barbara M. Joosse (Chronicle, 1991)

Merry Christmas, Little Critter! by Mercer Mayer (HarperFestival, 2004)

Me Too! by Mercer Mayer (Random House, 1996)

Mike Mulligan and His Steam Shovel by Virginia Lee Burton (Houghton Mifflin, 1939)

Miss Bindergarten Gets Ready for Kindergarten by Joseph Slate (Puffin, 2001)

Miss Bindergarten Stays Home from Kindergarten by Joseph Slate (Puffin, 2000)

Miss Spider's Tea Party by David Kirk (Scholastic, 1994)

The Mitten by Jan Brett (Putnam Juvenile, 1989)

Molly's Pilgrim by Barbara Cohen (HarperCollins, 1995)

Monster Goes to School by Virginia Mueller (Albert Whitman & Company, 1991)

More More More Said the Baby by Vera B. Williams (HarperTrophy, 1990)

Mosquitoes by Cheryl Coughlan (Capstone Press, 1999)

My Brown Bear Barney by Dorothy Butler (Greenwillow Books, 1989)

My Friends by Taro Gami (Chronicle, 1990)

My Picture Dictionary by Diane Snowball and Robyn Greene (Mondo, 1994)

Nana Upstairs Nana Downstairs by Tomie dePaola (Putnam Juvenile, 1973)

The New Baby by Mercer Mayer (Random House, 2001)

The Night Before Kindergarten by Natasha Wing (Grosset & Dunlap, 2001)

The Night Before Valentine's Day by Natasha Wing (Grosset & Dunlap, 2001)

Nine Days to Christmas: A Story of Mexico by Marie Hall Ets and Aurora Labastida (Puffin, 1991)

Oink! Moo! How Do You Do? A Book of Animal Sounds by Grace Maccarone (Scholastic, 1994)

Old MacDonald Had a Farm by Jane Cabrera (Holiday House, 2008)

The Old Man's Mitten by Yevonne Pollock (Mondo, 1994)

The 100th Day of School by Angela Shelf Medearis (Cartwheel, 1996)

On Market Street by Arnold Lobel (HarperTrophy, 1964)

On the Go by Ann Morris (HarperTrophy, 1994)

One Fish Two Fish Red Fish Blue Fish by Dr. Seuss (Random House, 1960)

One Tough Turkey by Steven Kroll (Holiday House, 1982)

Over in the Meadow by Ezra Jack Keats (Puffin, 1999)

Owen's Marshmallow Chick by Kevin Henkes (HarperCollins, 2002)

Owl Moon by Jane Yolen (Philomel, 1987)

Ox-Cart Man by Donald Hall (Puffin, 1979)

Pilgrims of Plymouth by Susan Goodman (National Geographic Children's Books, 1999)

References ···

Polar Bear, Polar Bear, What Do You Hear? by Bill Martin Jr. (Puffin, 1991)

The Popcorn Book by Tomie dePaola (Holiday House, 1984)

Potluck by Anne Shelby (Scholastic, 1993)

Pretend You're a Cat by Jean Marzollo (Dial, 1990)

Put Me in the Zoo by Robert Lopshire (Random House, 1960)

Rain by Robert Kalan (HarperTrophy, 1991)

The Real Mother Goose (Rand McNally & Company, 1916)

The Relatives Came by Cynthia Rylant (Aladdin, 1985)

Roaring Rockets by Tony Mitton and Ant Parker (Kingfisher, 2000)

Rosie's Walk by Pat Hutchins (Aladdin, 1968)

"Rub a Dub, Dub, Three Men in a Tub" (public domain)

School Bus by Donald Crews (HarperTrophy, 1987)

School Days by B. G. Hennessy (Puffin, 1990)

The Seasons of Arnold's Apple Tree by Gail Gibbons (Voyager, 1988)

The Secret Birthday Message by Eric Carle (HarperTrophy, 1971)

Seven Spools of Thread by Angela Shelf Medearis (Albert Whitman and Company, 2000)

Sheep on a Ship by Nancy Shaw (Houghton Mifflin, 1989)

Sleepy ABC by Margaret Wise Brown (HarperCollins, 1994)

The Snowy Day by Ezra Jack Keats (Viking, 1962)

Song and Dance Man by Karen Ackerman (Knopf Books for Young Readers, 1988)

The Story of Ferdinand by Munro Leaf (Scholastic, 1964)

Summer Stinks by Marty Kelley (Zino Press Children's Books, 2001)

Ten Apples Up on Top! by Dr. Seuss (Random House, 1961)

10 Fat Turkeys by Tony Johnson (Cartwheel, 2004)

Ten in the Bed by Jane Cabrera (Holiday House, 2006)

Terrific Trains by Tony Mitton and Ant Parker (Kingfisher, 2000)

Thanksgiving Day by Gail Gibbons (Holiday House, 1985)

There's a Bug in My Mug by Kent Salisbury (Learning Horizons, 1997)

There's a Wocket in My Pocket by Dr. Seuss (Random House, 1974)

Things I Like by Anthony Browne (Dragonfly Books, 1989)

Timothy Goes to School by Rosemary Wells (Puffin, 1981)

Today Is Thanksgiving by P. K. Hallinan (Ideals Publications, 1993)

"To Market, To Market" (public domain)

Too Many Tamales by Gary Soto and Ed Martinez (Putnam Juvenile, 1993)

Tough Trucks by Tony Mitton and Ant Parker (Kingfisher, 2005)

Trains by Lola M. Schaefer (Heinemann, 2003)

Tremendous Tractors by Tony Mitton and Ant Parker (Kingfisher, 2005)

'Twas the Night Before Christmas by Clement C. Moore (public domain)

Two Eyes, a Nose, and a Mouth by Roberta Grobel Intrater (Scholastic, 2000)

Valentine's Day by Miriam Nerlove (Albert Whitman & Company, 1994)

Vegetable Garden by Douglas Florian (Voyager, 1991)

The Very Busy Spider by Eric Carle (Penguin, 1984)

The Very Hungry Caterpillar by Eric Carle (Penguin, 1987)

Watch Out for the Chicken Feet in Your Soup by Tomie dePaola (Aladdin, 1974)

We Can Share at School by Rozanne Lanczak Williams (Creative Teaching Press, 1996)

The Wedding by Eve Bunting (Charlesbridge, 2005)

We're Going on a Bear Hunt by Michael Rosen (Aladdin, 1993)

What Is Thanksgiving? by Harriet Ziefert (HarperCollins, 1992)

What Will the Weather Be Like Today? by Paul Rogers (Scholastic, 1989)

What's in My Pocket? by Rozanne Lanczak Williams (Creative Teaching Press, 1994)

The Wheels on the Bus by Raffi (Crown Books for Young Readers, 1990)

When I Get Bigger by Mercer Mayer (Random House, 1999)

References ···

When I Grow Up by Babs Bell Hajdusiewicz (Dominie Press, 1996)

When It Snows by JoAnne Nelson (Modern Curriculum Press, 1993)

Where Does the Butterfly Go When It Rains? by May Garelick (Mondo, 1961)

Where the Wild Things Are by Maurice Sendak (HarperCollins, 1963)

White Is the Moon by Valerie Greeley (Atheneum, 1991)

White Rabbit's Color Book by Alan Baker (Kingfisher Books, 1994)

Who Said Red? by Mary Serfozo (Aladdin Books, 1992)

Winter: Discovering the Seasons by Louis Santrey (Troll Communications, 1983)

Wonders of Plants and Flowers by Laura Damon (Troll Associates, 1990)

Yertle the Turtle and Other Stories by Dr. Seuss (Random House, 1958)

You Can Do It, Sam by Amy Hest (Candlewick, 2003)

You're All My Favorites by Sam McBratney (Candlewick, 2004)

Zoo-Looking by Mem Fox (Mondo, 1996)

Professional References

An Observation Survey of Early Literacy Achievement by Marie Clay (Heinemann, 1997)

"Applying a Compare/Contrast Process to Identifying Polysyllabic Words" by Patricia Cunningham, *Journal of Reading Behavior*, 12, pp. 213–223 (1980)

Beginning to Read: Thinking and Learning about Print by Marilyn Jager Adams (MIT Press, 1990)

Building Blocks "Plus" for Kindergarten Bulletin Board (Carson-Dellosa, 1998)

"A Compare/Contrast Theory of Mediated Word Identification" by Patricia Cunningham *The Reading Teacher*, 32, pp. 774–778 (1979)

"The Effects of Rime–Based Analogy Training on Word Reading and Spelling of First–Grade Students with Good and Poor Phonological Awareness" by L. H. Davis (Doctoral dissertation, Northwestern University, 2000). *Dissertation Abstracts International*, 61, 2253 A

"Emergent Literacy" by Elizabeth Sulzby and William M. Teale. *Handbook of Reading Research, Vol. II* (1991)

"Everything You Wanted to Know about Phonics (but Were Afraid to Ask)" by S. A. Stahl, A. M. Duffy-Hester, and K. A. Stahl. *Reading Research Quarterly, 33, pp. 338–355* (1998)

Findings of the National Reading Panel. Testimony before the U.S. Senate Appropriations Committee's Subcommittee on Labor, Health and Human Services, and Education by D. N. Langenberg. (2000, April 13) *http://www.readingrockets.org/article.php?ID=254*

"Focusing Attention on Decoding for Students with Poor Reading Skills: Design and Preliminary Tests of the Word Building Intervention" by B. McCandliss, I. L. Beck, R. Sandak, and C. Perfetti, *Scientific Studies of Reading, 7, pp. 75–104* (2003)

Interactive Charts by Dorothy Hall and Karen Loman (Carson-Dellosa, 2002)

"Investigating a Synthesized Theory of Mediated Word Identification" by Patricia Cunningham *Reading Research Quarterly, 11, pp. 127–143* (1975–76)

Learning Centers in Kindergarten by Karen Loman and Dorothy Hall (Carson-Dellosa, 2004)

Every Child Reading: A Professional Development Guide (Learning First Alliance, 2000)

"Learning How to Read Words: Linguistic Units and Instructional Strategies" by C. Juel and C. Minden-Cupp. *Reading Research Quarterly, 35, pp. 458–492* (2000)

"Literature Based Reading Instruction" by Leslie Morrow and Linda Gambrell in M. L. Kamil, P. B. Mosenthal, P. D. Pearson, and R. Barr (Eds.) *Handbook of Reading Research, Vol. III, pp. 563–586* (2000)

References ·

"Literacy Knowledge in Practice: Contexts of Participation for Young Writers and Readers" by Susan Neuman and Kathleen Roskos. *Reading Research Quarterly*, 32(1), pp. 10–32 (1997)

Making Alphabet Books to Teach Letters and Sounds by Dorothy Hall (Carson-Dellosa, 2002)

Phonemic Awareness Songs and Rhymes: Fall by Kimberly Jordano and Trisha Callella (Creative Teaching Press, 1998)

Phonics They Use: Words for Reading and Writing by Patricia Cunningham (Longman, 2000)

Predictable Charts by Dorothy Hall and Elaine Williams (Carson-Dellosa, 2002)

Put Reading First by Bonnie Armbruster, Fran Lehr, and Jean Osborne (National Institute of Literacy, 2001)

Spel . . . Is a Four Letter Word by J. Richard Gentry (Heinemann, 1987)

Teaching Students to Read: An Evidence-Based Assessment of the Scientific Research Literature on Reading and Its Implications for Reading Instruction: Reports of the Subgroups. National Reading Panel, National Institute of Health Publication Number 00–4754. (National Institute of Child Health and Human Development, 2000)

"Teaching Decoding Skills to Educable Mentally Handicapped Students" by Patricia Cunningham and F. M. Guthrie. *The Reading Teacher*, 35, pp. 554–559 (1982)

Teaching Students to Spell by J. Richard Gentry and Jean Wallace Gillet (Heinemann, 1993)

"What Kind of Phonics Instruction Will We Have?" by Patricia Cunningham. *National Reading Conference Yearbook*, 41, pp. 17–31 (1992)

"You Can Analyze Developmental Spelling—And Here's How To Do It!" by J. Richard Gentry. *Early Years K–8* (1985)

Notes ··